GATS: The Case for Open Services Markets

OECD

ORGANISATION FOR ECONOMIC CO-OPERATION AND DEVELOPMENT

ORGANISATION FOR ECONOMIC CO-OPERATION AND DEVELOPMENT

Pursuant to Article 1 of the Convention signed in Paris on 14th December 1960, and which came into force on 30th September 1961, the Organisation for Economic Co-operation and Development (OECD) shall promote policies designed:

- to achieve the highest sustainable economic growth and employment and a rising standard of living in Member countries, while maintaining financial stability, and thus to contribute to the development of the world economy;
- to contribute to sound economic expansion in Member as well as non-member countries in the process of economic development; and
- to contribute to the expansion of world trade on a multilateral, non-discriminatory basis in accordance with international obligations.

The original Member countries of the OECD are Austria, Belgium, Canada, Denmark, France, Germany, Greece, Iceland, Ireland, Italy, Luxembourg, the Netherlands, Norway, Portugal, Spain, Sweden, Switzerland, Turkey, the United Kingdom and the United States. The following countries became Members subsequently through accession at the dates indicated hereafter: Japan (28th April 1964), Finland (28th January 1969), Australia (7th June 1971), New Zealand (29th May 1973), Mexico (18th May 1994), the Czech Republic (21st December 1995), Hungary (7th May 1996), Poland (22nd November 1996), Korea (12th December 1996) and the Slovak Republic (14th December 2000). The Commission of the European Communities takes part in the work of the OECD (Article 13 of the OECD Convention).

Publié en français sous le titre :

Pour l'ouverture des marchés de services

L'ACCORD GÉNÉRAL SUR LE COMMERCE DES SERVICES

Foreword

For more than a decade, services have been the fastest growing component of the global economy. Total measurable trade in services, as defined by the various "modes of supply" subject to multilateral disciplines under the World Trade Organisation's General Agreement on Trade in Services (GATS), stand at some USD 2.3 trillion today. This represents 7.6% of world output and close to a fifth of total trade in goods and services. Such figures are useful reminders of the economic and commercial significance of the sector and of negotiations aimed at progressively rolling back impediments to trade and investment in services.

In virtually every country the performance of the services economy, particularly the key enabling sectors of finance, telecommunications and transportation, can make the difference between rapid and sluggish growth. Simply put, an inefficient service sector acts like a prohibitive tax on a national economy. Growing realisation of the economy-wide potential of efficient service industries ushered in far-reaching liberalisation of trade and investment and efforts at regulatory reform throughout the world in recent years, facilitating attempts to anchor such reforms in international agreements governing cross-border trade and investment.

The GATS ranks without a doubt amongst the chief accomplishments of multilateral trade diplomacy at the end of the 20th century. Yet the agreement lies at the centre of the controversies surrounding trade policy at the start of the 21st.

Services encompass a vast and disparate array of economic activity and imply a similarly wide scope of issues, institutions and interests. Much as the first set of services talks during the Uruguay Round elicited relatively little attention and public scrutiny beyond the *cognoscenti* in academic, governmental and private-sector circles, proposals to build upon the achievements of the Uruguay Round and subsequent negotiations in the World Trade Organisation (WTO) command considerable attention today, not all of it positive.

Critical assessments of the GATS typically find their origin in the broader context of backlash against globalisation and the commercialisation that it brings to some activities previously insulated from the market. Claims of threats to the provision of public services, such as education or health services, or to services with strong public good connotations, such as water or electricity distribution, are among the most commonly voiced concerns associated with the GATS and with the very idea of liberalisation of trade and investment in services, including at regional level.

A paradox of anti-GATS sentiment is that much of it is rooted in the OECD area, where the share of services in employment and standards of living is highest and where the benefits of regulatory reform and of liberalisation of trade and investment in services have arguably generated the greatest gains in consumer welfare and allocative efficiencies. Not surprisingly, the public policy debate on services in OECD countries has not tended to centre on disputing the economic case for open markets. Rather, the criticism has generally focused on the respective roles that the market and the state (as both regulator and direct purveyor of services such as education and health) should assume, as well on the perceived threat to national regulatory sovereignty allegedly posed by trade and investment rule-making.

Many of the arguments put forward today against liberalisation of trade and investment in services are based on misinformation and a lack of understanding of the GATS. At the same time, the significant economy-wide benefits deriving from liberalisation of trade and investment in services do not receive enough attention, and this reinforces less than positive views of the liberalisation of trade and investment in general and participation in the multilateral trading system through membership of the WTO in particular.

Mindful of the need to restore greater balance to this nascent public policy debate, Member countries asked the OECD Trade Directorate in early 2001 to prepare a study aimed at helping governments to better communicate the economic rationale for committing to – and maintaining – open services markets and to identify more clearly what is and what is not at stake in the new set of WTO services negotiations.

The present study, which follows in the footsteps of the Organisation's highly acclaimed 1998 *Open Markets Matter*, is the answer to that request. It reviews the most recent empirical evidence in order to offer a comprehensive treatment of the benefits and costs of liberalisation of trade and investment in services. It also provides an in-depth consideration of – and offers a counter narrative to – some of the most prominent criticisms levelled at the GATS and the pursuit of liberalisation of trade and investment in services.

This study explains why the GATS, far from the sovereignty-impairing straightjacket that its critics claim, can in many regards be seen as the most "development-friendly" of all WTO agreements, affording member countries full freedom to choose the nature, pace and form of market opening in a multilateral setting. It shows why the gains from international co-operation and multilateral rule-making are particularly large in the services area. Because such gains have just begun to be tapped, the ongoing negotiations, to which the Doha Development Agenda has given renewed impetus, offers WTO members a ready-made opportunity to use the GATS as a means to support domestic reforms deemed beneficial from a development perspective by governments and civil society.

This study, which forms part of the OECD Trade Committee's ongoing work programme on trade in services, was drafted by Pierre Sauvé of the Trade Directorate. It benefitted from significant contributions by Rosemary Morris and Massimo Geloso-Grosso and drew on background documentation prepared by Craig van Grasstek.

This volume is published on the responsibility of the Secretary-General of the OECD.

Acronyms

ABT	Agreement on Basic Telecommunications
APEC	Asia-Pacific Economic Cooperation Forum
CGE	Computable general equilibrium
DSU	Dispute Settlement Understanding (WTO)
ESM	Emergency safeguard measure
FDI	Foreign direct investment
GATS	General Agreement on Trade in Services
GATT	General Agreement on Tariffs and Trade
GDP	Gross domestic product
GPA	Government Procurement Agreement (WTO)
ICT	Information and communication technologies
ILO	International Labour Organization
IMF	International Monetary Fund
ITU	International Telecommunications Union
MAI	Multilateral Agreement on Investment
MFN	Most favoured nation
NAFTA	North American Free Trade Agreement
SCM	Subsidies and Countervailing Measures (WTO)
UNCTAD	United Nations Conference on Trade and Development
WTO	World Trade Organization

Table of Contents

Boxes

Figures

Tables

Executive Summary

Despite the failure of World Trade Organization (WTO) members to launch a new round at the 3rd Ministerial Conference held in Seattle in November 1999, negotiations under the General Agreement on Trade in Services (GATS) formally resumed on 1 January 2000, as foreseen under the Uruguay Round's so-called "built-in" agenda. As the services negotiations have progressed, the GATS has become the focus of civil society groups representing a wide range of interests. Arguments against the GATS concern principally the threat it is alleged to pose to countries' sovereign right to regulate the production, sale, distribution or import of services and to supply services. For the most part, these claims are based on misunderstandings which this publication aims to address. Still, concerns about the GATS, its effect on public services, its implications for national sovereignty and governments' ability to regulate are genuine and need to be addressed. The new negotiating round provides a ready-made opportunity for governments to inform concerned constituencies about the GATS and its impact on national economic and social goals. To serve a useful purpose, however, the public policy debate must be based on facts, not on misconceptions.

This study has a threefold purpose. First, to recall the economic case for service sector reform and the policy rationales for pursuing open services markets through liberalisation of trade and investment. Second, to address concerns over the effects of the GATS by explaining how the Agreement operates, the obligations WTO Members subscribe to and the policy options they may pursue under the Agreement. Third, to point out some of the key negotiating challenges of the current GATS round, with particular attention to the interests and concerns of developing countries, and the potential of the GATS for anchoring development-enhancing reforms in services markets.

Services are essential inputs in the production of goods and other services. They encompass a vast and disparate range of economic activities and dominate the economies of developed and many developing countries. A strong case can be made in support of regulatory reform efforts and liberalisation of trade and investment in the services context. There are many current examples of economy-wide as well as sectoral benefits arising directly from trade liberalisation and investment. This has been the case for goods trade since the creation of the

General Agreement on Tariffs and Trade (GATT) in 1947. It is equally pertinent for services today. Indeed, the economic rationale underlying the GATT, and the subsequent progressive liberalisation of merchandise trade over more than five decades, is in all likelihood even more compelling in the services context. An inefficient service sector acts like a prohibitive tax on a national economy. Open services markets bring direct economy-wide benefits by facilitating and encouraging innovation, efficiency and improved quality. When they are regulated in accordance with sound, efficiency-enhancing principles, open trade and investment regimes provide the best opportunity for wider (and informed) consumer choice and better quality products. They can also reduce the scope for wasteful use of resources and rent-seeking, constrain the power of individual economic operators and enhance overall economic performance.

Services are one area where the potential gains from international co-operation and multilateral rule-making are large and where the benefits of such co-operation have barely begun to be tapped. Empirical assessments of services policy reform in developing countries reveal positive economy-wide benefits flowing from the removal of inefficiencies. Such benefits are in fact quite large relative to what is usually found in empirical assessments of the impact of merchandise trade liberalisation. The benefits from continued services reform and liberalisation, while undoubtedly larger in relative terms for developing countries, are by no means negligible for OECD countries. Indeed, empirical studies point to a number of favourable economy-wide outcomes in those OECD countries where regulatory reform in service industries have gone further in enhancing competition.

Still, there is no denying that, as in the case of merchandise trade, liberalisation of services markets may be associated with displacement and adjustment difficulties. For this reason, the liberalisation process must be well managed, rest on sound regulatory underpinnings, pursued in a progressive manner and feature policies that mitigate potentially adverse social and economic consequences arising from the adjustment process.

The GATS consists of three major elements: the framework that lays out the general obligations for services trade, in much the same way as the GATT does for trade in goods; a number of annexes on specific sectors as well as the schedules of commitments submitted by WTO Members. Due to its structure and its selective "bottom-up" approach to liberalisation, the GATS allows WTO Members to select the sectors, modes of supply and regulatory conditions in which liberalisation commitments are made. They may also leave entire sectors for which they make no commitments out of their schedules. Such flexibility, and the emphasis placed on the progressive, voluntary nature of liberalisation, help explain why the GATS is arguably the most "development-friendly" of all Uruguay Round Agreements. Unlike the GATT, the GATS is still a new agreement, not yet complete, with much unfinished rule-making business to be tackled.

An agreement to accept a framework of rules, whether bilateral, plurilateral or multilateral, entails by definition some curtailment of sovereignty, although the decision to enter into such an agreement is itself an exercise of sovereignty. Through their membership in the WTO, however, over 140 governments have chosen to participate in a package of multilateral agreements because they recognise the overall net economic and social benefits that accrue from a rules-based trading system. Under the GATS, governments retain the right to: schedule their commitments so as to regulate with a view to pursuing national policy objectives; modify and/or withdraw commitments undertaken; designate or maintain monopolies, public or private; choose the sectors for which they want to grant access and the conditions governing such access. In short, the GATS permits member countries to undertake the progressive opening of service sectors and integration into the multilateral trading system at their own pace and in accordance with their national priorities and objectives.

Criticism of the GATS typically finds its origin in the broader context of backlash against globalisation and the commercialisation of certain activities previously insulated from the market. Claims of threats to the provision of public services, such as education or health services, or to services with strong "public good" connotations, such as water or electricity distribution, are among the most commonly voiced concerns associated with the GATS and with the very idea of liberalisation of trade and investment in services (including that pursued at regional level). Such claims are often based on the premise that the GATS threatens the democratic provision of essential services, or even democracy itself. In effect, some of the criticism, while nominally directed at the GATS and the WTO, can be seen as warnings to national governments that the terms of the domestic social contract should be negotiated at national – and not supranational – level.

Threats to a country's right to regulate, or the alleged transfer of regulatory authority from national governments to a supranational body such as the WTO, is a central plank of anti-GATS criticism. A common mistake in the GATS debate is to use the terms "liberalisation" and "deregulation" interchangeably, as if they were synonyms. They are not, and it is simply wrong to assimilate regulations to trade restrictions. Liberalisation of services, indeed, often necessitates regulation or re-regulation. But this does not imply that regulation, whether for economic or social purposes, cannot be designed, implemented or enforced in more transparent and efficient ways, with positive overall effects in terms of democratic governance.

A paradox of anti-GATS sentiment is that much of it is rooted in the OECD area, where the share of services in employment and standards of living are highest, and where the benefits of regulatory reform and of liberalisation of trade and investment in services have arguably generated the greatest gains in consumer welfare and allocative efficiencies. Not surprisingly, the public policy debate on services in OECD countries has not tended to centre on disputing the economic case for open markets. Rather, criticism of the GATS has generally focused on the respective roles that the market and the state (as both regulator and direct purveyor of services such as education and health) should assume, as well as on the perceived threat to national regulatory sovereignty allegedly posed by trade and investment rule-making.

This agenda differs quite significantly from that in many developing countries, where the reluctance to embrace liberalisation of trade and investment in services in a GATS setting – even as such liberalisation is increasingly practised domestically – can be traced to a combination of factors. These include tactical bargaining considerations in the WTO as well as the power of vested interests in government and in import-competing sectors. However, it also reflects the legitimate concerns of many developing countries regarding their lack of appropriate regulatory regimes and institutions, weak technical capacities, poor market information, difficulties in meeting product standards in export markets, and the need for significant upgrading of human resources. All these ingredients are required to make a success of liberalisation, and their absence or relative paucity may constrain the ability of many developing countries to supply services in export markets, even where a demand for such services may exist (UNCTAD, 1999*a*).

The multilateral community faces a dual challenge in the current GATS round. The first consists of responding credibly to the rising chorus of criticisms levelled at the GATS. There can be little doubt that even as such concerns are legitimately felt and expressed, they are in many instances greatly exaggerated and demonstrate a misunderstanding of the aims and *modus operandi* of the GATS. This study identifies, and supplies a counter-narrative to, some of the key misunderstandings arising in the controversy surrounding the GATS.

A second challenge is to build support among all WTO members, and especially developing countries, for wider and more commercially meaningful GATS commitments and to encourage countries to use the Agreement more readily as a means of anchoring – and giving investment-attracting permanency to – domestic reform efforts. Liberalisation under the GATS will nonetheless remain progressive in character, and will in many instances require concomitant efforts at capacity-building in education, training, institutional and regulatory matters for which funding and technical assistance will be required in larger doses than those on offer to date. To make a success of the GATS negotiations, efforts will be needed to progressively open up areas of export interest to developing countries, notably in sectors such as construction, computer and related services, tourism and travel-related activities, as well as in respect of the movement of natural persons, so-called "mode 4" trade in services.

Chapter 1

Introduction

The General Agreement on Trade in Services (GATS) ranks among the chief accomplishments of multilateral trade diplomacy at the end of the 20th century, but is at the centre of the controversies surrounding trade policy at the start of the 21st. The share of services in world economic activity has expanded markedly in recent years. In the OECD area, services dominate the economic landscape of advanced economies, accounting for close to 70% of production and employment. However, the share of services has increased particularly strongly in developing countries. A recent World Bank study found that while the share of services in world GDP increased by five percentage points between 1980 and 1998, the corresponding increase for low and middle-income countries was nine percentage points, an indication of far-reaching structural changes in their domestic economies (World Bank, 1999).

Services encompass a vast and disparate array of economic activities, and imply a similarly wide scope of issues, institutions and interests. The first round of multilateral negotiations in the area attracted relatively little attention and public scrutiny beyond the *cognoscenti* in academic, governmental and private-sector circles, Today, however, proposals to build upon the achievements of the Uruguay Round and subsequent negotiations in the World Trade Organisation (WTO) command considerable attention, not all of it positive.

Negotiations on the GATS began on 1 January 2000 as part of the Uruguay Round's so-called "built-in" agenda. As the services negotiations have progressed, civil society groups representing a wide range of interests – environmentalists, anti-free traders, those who oppose globalisation, trade unions – are finding a common target in the GATS. However, many of the arguments being put forward today against liberalisation of trade and investment in services are based on misinformation and a lack of understanding of the GATS. At the same time, the significant economy-wide benefits deriving from liberalisation of trade and investment in services are not getting sufficient "airplay", a factor that reinforces less than positive conceptions about liberalisation of trade and investment in general, and participation in the multilateral trading system through membership of the WTO in particular.

This study has a threefold purpose. First, it recalls the economic case for service sector reform and the policy rationales for pursuing open service markets through liberalisation of trade and investment. Second, it aims to address concerns over the alleged effects of the GATS by explaining how the Agreement operates and the obligations WTO Members subscribe to and the policy options they may pursue under the Agreement. Third, it addresses the interests of developing countries in the current GATS negotiations and the Agreement 's potential for anchoring development-enhancing reforms in services markets.

As the study's title implies, a strong case can be made in support of efforts to liberalise trade and investment in the services context, as Chapter 2 argues. There are many current examples of economy-wide as well as sectoral benefits arising directly from liberalisation of trade and investment. This has been the case for goods trade since the creation of the General Agreement on Tariffs and Trade (GATT) in 1947. It is equally pertinent for services today. Indeed, the economic rationale underlying the GATT and the progressive liberalisation of merchandise trade over more than five decades is in all likelihood even more compelling in the services context. Open services markets bring direct economy-wide benefits by facilitating and encouraging innovation, efficiency and improved quality. When they are regulated in accordance with sound, efficiency-enhancing principles, open trade and investment regimes provide the best opportunity for wider (and informed) consumer choice and better quality products, reduce the scope for wasteful resource use and rent-seeking, constrain the power of individual economic operators and enhance overall economic performance.

Chapter 3 draws attention to the economy-wide importance of service sector efficiency. It recalls that many services are essential inputs into the production of goods and other services. In this context, it is important to note the critical role of infrastructure services, given that efficient services in the areas of transport, communications, finance, energy or distribution hold the key to enhancing the productivity and growth of the entire economy. An inefficient service sector acts like a prohibitive tax on a national economy. Liberalisation of trade and investment conditions in these sectors has led to substantial and tangible social and economic gains, particularly in developing countries where core infrastructures were in need of significant upgrading and innovation. The study draws on available empirical studies to explain, through examples and the available data, the benefits of market openness for services. These benefits accrue to: individual consumers; employees who, contrary to popular belief, tend in most service sectors to earn higher wages than in manufacturing; small and medium-sized enterprises (SMEs), both as consumers and suppliers of services; other service providers; producers in other sectors (*e.g.* user industries); and society as a whole.

There is no denying that, as with goods trade, the liberalisation of services markets may sometimes be associated with displacement and adjustment difficulties. This calls for proper sequencing in the design of liberalisation and adjustment strategies and for government support measures aimed at mitigating adjustment problems at the source. Following Chapter 3, a special section summarises the findings of a number of recent empirical studies on the effects of liberalisation of trade and investment in services. Next, Chapter 4, which considers the complexities of services reforms, stresses that well-managed trade liberalisation programmes are those that proceed with liberalisation in a progressive, orderly and adjustment-promoting manner, providing mechanisms, policies and institutions for easing any such negative social and economic consequences.

Chapter 5 examines the nature of the criticisms directed against the GATS, noting that these are often elements in the broader context of reaction against the far-reaching changes associated with the process of globalisation. Technological developments that enable us to think in terms of a "borderless world" assuredly lie behind this process, but other factors are important as well, including enhanced economic links between countries, a far-reaching reassessment of the role of governments, the appearance of new markets and alliances, to name just a few. These changes do not come without a displacement of the traditional order, difficulties of adaptation and social costs. An increasingly globalised environment can give rise to concerns over the ability of governments to protect labour markets, manage natural resources or promote the health of citizens. The ensuing resistance often translates into resistance to market openness and calls to slow the pace of change.

However, the actual links between liberalisation of trade and investment, exemplified in WTO agreements (but also originating from other, subsidiary, sources, such as regional and bilateral agreements as well as unilateral liberalisation and regulatory reform efforts), and the putative downsides often attributed to liberalisation are rarely explained or backed up by comprehensive empirical evidence. Misunderstandings tend, in many instances, to flow from anecdotal evidence on which broad generalisations are made. At the same time, the anti-GATS discourse tends to leave aside the net social and economic benefits that liberalisation of trade and investment has brought to developed and developing countries alike.

The present study's overview of the globalisation debate emphasises that more is at issue than a simple matter of scale. The inclusion of new activities within the scope of market disciplines is a perennial source of controversy, whether the market is domestic or international. This study stresses that liberalisation of services markets is already well under way with or without the GATS, and is being propelled both by new technological applications and by the autonomous – and typically pro-liberalising – policy decisions of national governments. New negotiations in the GATS should help not only to codify the high level of *de facto* liberalisation that has been achieved in recent years, including in the short period since the end of the Uruguay Round, but also to encourage countries to exchange mutually beneficial commitments to open their markets further. In this way, the WTO can help ensure that the needed process of adjustment to changing social and economic realities is pursued in a progressive, orderly manner.

Chapters 6 and 7 focus on the GATS itself, recalling the objectives and operation of the Agreement and addressing some of the principal misconceptions in the public debate over the GATS and its alleged effects on the ability of sovereign governments to regulate service sectors in order to pursue national policy goals. Much of the current public debate over the alleged downsides of liberalisation of trade and investment in services is rooted in misunderstandings about the complex geometry of the GATS and of trade in services more generally. By explaining the relevant provisions of the GATS text, the study aims to respond to some of the principal claims being made about it. In particular, it seeks to provide factual information and explanations as to the nature and scope of the GATS "carve-out" for public services, its treatment of investment and its disciplines on domestic regulation. It explains how, rather than undermining sovereignty, the GATS explicitly recognises the right of governments to regulate in order to pursue national policy objectives. In particular, the GATS allows a great deal of flexibility so that members can select the sectors, modes and conditions of market access for which they wish to make commitments. Under the GATS, WTO members can, if and when they choose, exempt specific sectors from liberalisation, set conditions or limits on the nature and pace of any domestically determined liberalisation, or even suspend or modify concessions that they have already made.

Chapter 8 features a discussion of some of the key liberalisation challenges of the GATS 2000 round. Particular attention is paid in this context to the negotiating interests and concerns of developing countries; The chapter recalls the potential of the GATS for anchoring development-enhancing reforms in service markets. Chapter 9 offers a few concluding remarks. There is an extensive bibliography.

Chapter 2

Stating the Case for Open Services Markets

The most recent phase of economic globalisation – epitomised by revolutionary advances in telecommunications and information technology and complemented by far-reaching changes in approaches to domestic regulation and sweeping (and often unilateral) liberalisation of trade and foreign direct investment (FDI) regimes – has to a significant degree been driven by the internationalisation of services. In the process, many of the boundaries that used to distinguish tradable from non-tradable products – and indeed goods from services – have become blurred.

Such developments are of great importance to the growth and development prospects of all WTO members (see Box 1). The growing internationalisation of services and the greater ease with which services markets can now be contested worldwide, create opportunities for developing new sources of export growth. It also offers the prospect of importing a much broader range of producer services and technical know-how in a cost-effective manner.

To harness such opportunities, however, countries at all levels of development need to take up the challenge of improving efficiency in the provision of services. This is necessary not only to capture new export opportunities, for example in the realm of electronic commerce, but also because access to efficient services has become a key determinant of the overall competitiveness of national economies.

Trade in services: three waves of criticisms

The field of trade in services can be thought of as enduring the third major wave of criticism directed at it in the last quarter century. The first wave came in the late 1970s and early 1980s, when the topic was first mooted as fit for inclusion on the trade negotiating agenda. Neglect of tertiary activities is at least as old as economics itself, and those who were raised on the view that services are "invisibles" or the "non-traded sector" found it difficult to view them as sources of significant value added, productivity growth or trade benefits. Such views were soon dispelled when a series of groundbreaking empirical studies revealed both the

Box 1. Services in the global economy

Services, which include activities as diverse as the transportation of goods and people, financial intermediation, communications, distribution, accountancy, hotels and restaurants, education, health care and construction, account for a substantial and rising share of output in every economy. Even in the lowest-income countries, services account for more than a third of GDP. In middle-income countries, services generally account for more than 50% of output and a similar if not greater share of employment.*

While patterns of employment and production differ across countries for reasons of level of development, geographic location or resource endowment – economists have long observed that demand for services is relatively highly income elastic. Since the income elasticity of demand for services is also very high in comparison to that for other goods, as incomes grow and people become richer, their demand for services such as tourism, education and health expands more rapidly than that for manufactures or agricultural products. The growing share of services in GDP also reflects the ongoing organisational changes occurring in most economies. Manufacturing companies have tended increasingly to outsource services such as design, financing or transport, which they previously produced in house, and purchase them from specialised suppliers, domestic and foreign.

These changes help explain why services have been the fastest growing component of cross-border trade and investment (FDI) activity for the better part of the last decade and a half. Estimates show that total measurable trade in services, as defined by the various "modes of supply" subject to multilateral disciplines under the GATS, stood at some USD 2.3 trillion at the end of 2000. This represents 7.6% of world output and close to a fifth of total trade in goods and services (WTO, 2001*a*). Such figures are useful reminders of the economic and commercial significance of the sector and of negotiations aimed at progressively rolling back impediments to trade and investment in it.

Although OECD countries dominate global trade and investment in services, many developing countries are highly specialised in – and dependent on – services exports as a source of foreign exchange earnings. In most instances, this reflects the importance of activities related to tourism and travel. However, a growing number of developing countries are also becoming large exporters of transactions processing, back-office services and a burgeoning range of information and software development services. The potential to exploit recent and emerging technological developments that allow cross-border trade in services and provide firms with incentives to slice up the value chain geographically is enormous.

* Especially in developing economies, the size of the service sector is understated by employment and national income statistics. This is so because of the reliance on household production and the large size of the informal sector, which is usually dominated by services.

quantitative and qualitative significance of services.[1] As Figure 1 shows, the share of employment in services is a good proxy for an economy's level of development, as it tends to rise with per capita incomes. Moreover, some services have always been traded (*e.g.* shipping, tourism), while others that were once deemed non-tradable are now made internationally available through modern communications (*e.g.* business services). For most OECD countries, the value of service exports is between 20% and 30% of the value of their goods exports.

The second wave of criticism directed at services trade came in the mid-1980s, when developing countries initially balked at the proposal that services should be on the table at a new round of negotiations under the GATT. Policy makers from many developing countries feared that the industrialised countries' dominance in services would overwhelm their fledgling economies and threaten their capacity to control such sensitive areas as finance or telecommunications. These concerns have since diminished significantly, owing both to the development of a highly flexible, *à la carte* approach to liberalisation under the GATS (which developing countries were instrumental in crafting during the Uruguay Round), and to the growing realisation that developing countries can derive significant two-way benefits from more open trade in services, even where their principal source of

Figure 1. **Relationship between services employment and national income**

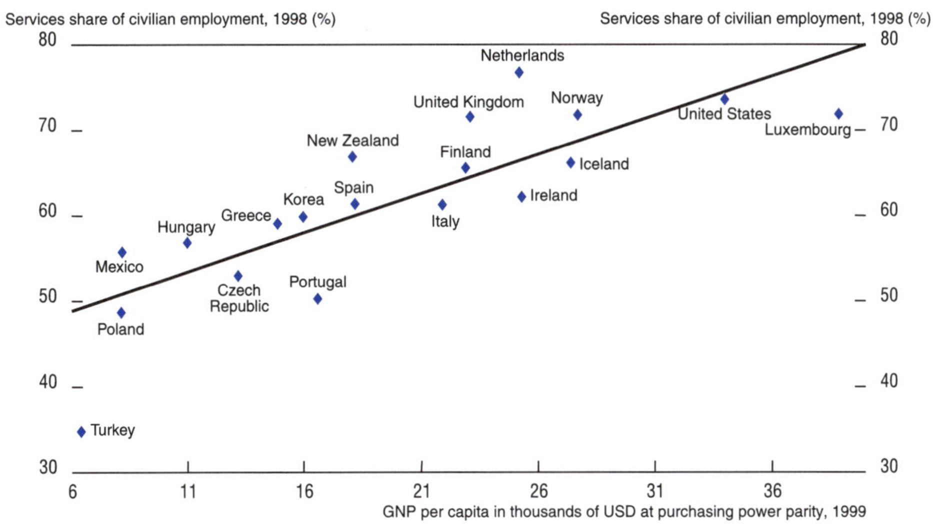

Note: Correlation coefficient = 0.80; R^2 = 0.64.
Source: Calculated from OECD data.

comparative advantage may lie in agriculture or manufacturing (Mattoo, 2000; Sauvé, 2000).

Such benefits take the form of reduced costs for imported intermediate services, which are typically critical inputs in the production of goods and other services, as well as of new export opportunities for developing countries' own service sectors. Figure 2 shows that while services once accounted for much more trade among industrialised countries than among developing countries, the gap has nearly disappeared. As Figure 3 reveals, services exports are not solely of interest to industrialised countries. Indeed, developing countries are today active *demandeurs* in services negotiations, especially in areas where they enjoy strong comparative advantages (*e.g.* tourism, labour mobility).

The third wave of criticism, which this study addresses, is the polar opposite of the first. Rather than seeing services as unproductive activities that are too insignificant to occupy the attention of trade policy makers, proponents of the most recent variant of anti-services talk argue that some service sectors are simply too important to be brought within the scope of international trade rules. This argument focuses on the threat that open trade in services allegedly poses for sensitive areas such as health, education and other social services, culture and utilities. According to some critics of the GATS, liberalisation of trade and

Figure 2. **Converging trends in services trade**
Share of services in total trade, 1980-2000

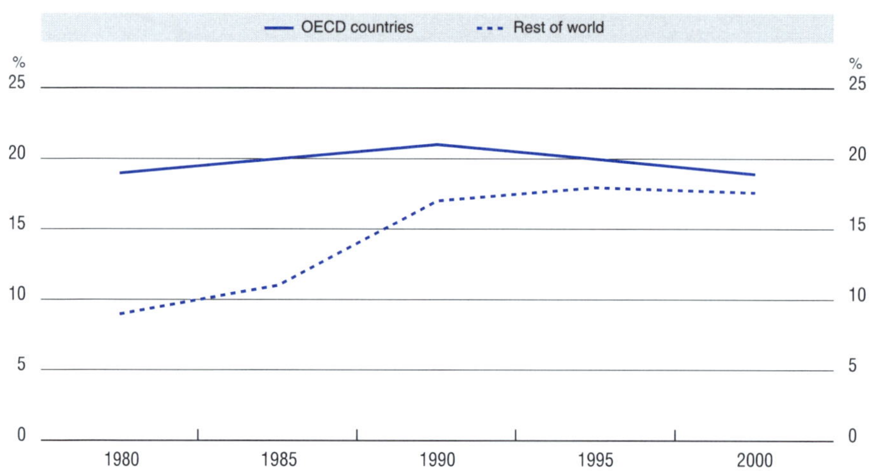

Source: Calculated from World Trade Organization data.

Figure 3. **Significance of services in selected countries' exports**
Commercial services exports as a share of total exports, 1999

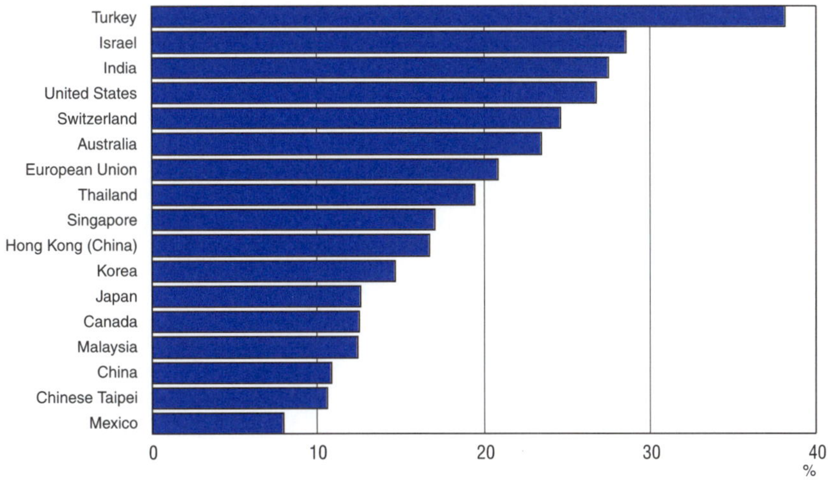

Source: Calculated from World Trade Organization (2000).

investment in services not only raises traditional concerns over the potentially injurious effects of competition on domestic producers, it also threatens to deny essential services to the poor, allows multinational corporations to dominate global markets, leads to the demise or marginalisation of indigenous cultures, menaces the health and well-being of consumers, undermines democracy and diminishes the regulatory sovereignty of states.

Such criticisms, however, demonstrate a misunderstanding of the GATS and its operation. One of the aims of this study is to address some of the concerns that lie behind this third wave of criticism and to put forward a number of arguments that will help to restore some balance to the nascent public policy controversy generated by a new round of GATS negotiations.

Chapter 3

Harnessing the Economy-wide Potential of Service Sector Efficiencies

The economic cost of protecting inefficient services is arguably of greater overall significance than that due to protectionism in the goods sector. Adopting a liberal trade and investment regime, and a pro-competitive regulatory stance in key infrastructural service sectors – telecommunications, finance, transport, energy – will be essential if countries are to maximise benefits from the internationalisation of services markets. Although the above-mentioned sectors are probably the most important for influencing a country's ability to participate in global trade, other services are also crucial. Business services such as accounting and legal services are particularly important for reducing transaction costs, the high level of which is often a major impediment to economic growth in developing countries. Education and health services are necessary for building up the stock of human capital. Retail and wholesale services are a vital link between producers and consumers and affect the efficiency with which resources are allocated to meet consumer needs. Computer and related services, including software development, are nothing less than the foundation of the modern knowledge-based economy. In addition, environmental services contribute to sustainable development by helping to alleviate the negative impact of economic activity on the environment (World Bank, 2001). Countries able to exploit these opportunities will find that the internationalisation of services can make a positive contribution to international economic convergence. In contrast, countries that fail to establish conditions conducive to the efficient provision of services run the very serious risk of falling further behind.

It should come as little surprise, then, that many countries, developed and developing, have in recent years undertaken far-reaching reforms targeted at increasing competition in domestic service sectors. To a significant extent, these reforms have been driven by changes in technologies that have facilitated the provision of services at much lower cost and allowed competition to emerge in markets that were traditionally regarded as natural monopolies. Service sector reforms have also been pushed by manufacturing and agricultural interests, as well as by downstream service "users", who have themselves faced greater international competition as barriers to trade and investment have been lowered.[2] Regardless of the individual measures or sectors involved, service sector reforms appear in most instances to be driven by one overriding objective: giving market forces a freer (but hardly ever unfettered) rein in determining production, trade and/or investment patterns. In turn, this objective has tended to imply a move towards competitive prices, aligned more closely on prevailing international levels, and additional emphasis on positive adjustments via product and process innovation and the transfer of best practices typically associated with open markets (WTO, 1998*a*).

The importance of policy in the service sector goes beyond the sector itself. Services are essential inputs into the production of virtually all other goods and services, and producers depend on services to deliver their output to end users. Because the price and quality of the services available in an economy have major impacts on all sectors, service sector policies and efficiency-enhancing reforms – including regulatory and institutional changes – can have major effects on overall economic performance. Accordingly, services liberalisation should not be viewed as a "concession" to other countries, but a precondition for enhancing domestic economic performance.

Producer services play an increasingly important role in the economies of all nations. Products are becoming increasingly time-sensitive, both because of shorter product life cycles and because of the pervasive use of "just-in-time" production management techniques. Foreign buyers must be assured that a supplier can deliver to specification and on time. For suppliers in developing countries to be competitive, they must be able to rely on efficient service industries that can provide inputs tailored to their needs. Restrictions on services trade and investment lead to service inputs of lower quality and higher cost. As a result, liberalisation can bring large efficiency and welfare gains.[3]

Recent efforts to quantify existing barriers, surveyed in Francois and Hoekman (1999), suggest that competition-inhibiting barriers tend to be relatively low in business services, consulting and distribution services as compared to barriers in transport, finance and telecommunications. The latter are basic "backbone" services that are crucial to the ability of enterprises to compete internationally. With the exception of transport, policies for these sectors appear to be significantly more restrictive in developing countries.[4]

The gains from liberalising services may be substantially greater than those from liberalising trade in goods. This is so both because current levels of protection are higher for the former and because liberalisation of services would also create additional spillover benefits from the associated movement of capital and labour. A number of country-specific exercises have been undertaken which demonstrate the economy-wide implications of policy reform in services in developing countries. Hoekman and Konan (1999), for instance, used a computable general equilibrium (CGE) model of Egypt to assess the orders of magnitude that may be involved in eliminating service sector inefficiencies. They showed that Egyptian output would rise by as much as 4% should service sectors become more open to competition. They also noted that the greater the extent to which regulatory and administrative practices give rise to resource costs (frictional or transaction costs), the greater the welfare improvement that would result from reform. A study by Konan and Maskus (2000) based on a CGE model of Tunisia showed that services liberalisation in six core sectors – telecommunications, construction, transportation, business and insurance, distribution and finance – could provide welfare gains equivalent to 7% of GDP. Such gains, the largest components of which result from the dismantling of barriers to FDI in financial services, telecommunications and transportation, are larger than the gains predicted to arise from Tunisia's preferential trade agreement with the European Union. Chadha (1999) used a multi-country CGE model which separated out India and ran simulations making different assumptions regarding prevailing market structures in agriculture, manufacturing and services. He concluded that Indian welfare would expand by 0.7% to 1.4% of GDP following a 25% global reduction in the assumed vector of services protection. His work also showed that other countries in South and Southeast Asia could expect efficiency gains of up to 3% of GDP.

Certain service industries clearly possess growth-generating characteristics. Econometric evidence – relatively strong for the financial sector and less strong, but still statistically significant for the telecommunications sector – suggests that openness in services can influence long-run growth performance. Recent work by Mattoo *et al.* (2001) showed that, after controlling for other influences on growth, countries that fully liberalised the financial service sector grew, on average, about 1 percentage point faster than other countries. An even greater impetus to growth – of the order of a 1.5% long-run growth premium – was found to flow from attempts to fully liberalise both the financial and telecommunications service sectors.[5]

Such results are quite large relative to what is usually found using similar types of models to assess the impact of merchandise trade liberalisation. They are strongly indicative of what many policy makers have long intuitively understood and demonstrated by a strong push towards unilateral liberalisation of their trade and investment regime for services: namely, the potentially significant economy-wide gains to be reaped from regulatory reform efforts and greater competition in service industries.

The benefits from continued services reform and liberalisation, while undoubtedly larger in relative terms for developing countries, are by no means negligible for OECD countries. Indeed, while OECD Member governments have over the past two decades extensively reformed regulatory environments in key service industries, initial regulatory conditions and the pace and extent of reform continue to differ markedly across countries. As a result, and as Table 1 and Figure 4 indicate, the dispersion of regulatory approaches within major service industries remains wide and gives large scope for further reform.

Table 1. **Regulatory environments in service industries and electricity supply in OECD countries**[1]

Legend: Very liberal · Liberal · Restrictive · Very restrictive

	Competitive industries				Network industries		
	Retail distribution	Road freight	Mobile telephony	Air passenger transport	Fixed telephony[2]	Electricity	Railways
Australia	Very liberal	Very liberal	Liberal	Liberal	Liberal	Very liberal	Very liberal
United States[3]	Very liberal	Very liberal	Liberal	Very liberal	Liberal	Restrictive	Very liberal
Sweden	Liberal	Liberal	Liberal	Liberal	Liberal	Very liberal	Liberal
United Kingdom	Restrictive	Very liberal	Liberal	Liberal	Liberal	Very liberal	Liberal
Germany	Liberal	Restrictive	Liberal	Liberal	Liberal	Liberal	Very liberal
Netherlands	Liberal	Restrictive	Liberal	Very liberal	Liberal	Restrictive	Very liberal
New Zealand	—	Very liberal	Very restrictive	Very liberal	Liberal	Very liberal	Very restrictive
Finland	Restrictive	Liberal	Liberal	Liberal	Liberal	Very liberal	Very restrictive
Norway	Restrictive	Liberal	Liberal	Liberal	Liberal	Very liberal	Very restrictive
Korea	Liberal	Very liberal	Liberal	Restrictive	Liberal	—	Very restrictive
Canada	Liberal	Liberal	—	Restrictive	Liberal	Very restrictive	Liberal
Ireland	Liberal	—	Liberal	Liberal	Liberal	Restrictive	Very restrictive
Mexico	Liberal	Liberal	Liberal	Restrictive	Liberal	—	Very restrictive
Iceland	Restrictive	—	Liberal	Restrictive	Liberal	—	
Denmark	Restrictive	—	Liberal	Liberal	Liberal	Restrictive	Very restrictive
Belgium	Restrictive	Restrictive	Liberal	Liberal	Liberal	Restrictive	Very restrictive
Japan[4]	Restrictive	Restrictive	Liberal	Restrictive	Liberal	Restrictive	Liberal
Austria	Very restrictive	Restrictive	Liberal	Liberal	Liberal	—	Very restrictive
France	Restrictive	Liberal	Liberal	Restrictive	Liberal	Very restrictive	Very restrictive
Switzerland	Very liberal	Very restrictive	Liberal	Very restrictive	Liberal	—	Very restrictive
Czech Republic	Very liberal	Restrictive	Very restrictive	Very restrictive	Very restrictive	—	Very liberal
Hungary	Liberal	Very restrictive	Very restrictive		Very restrictive	—	Very liberal
Portugal	Restrictive	Liberal	Liberal	Very restrictive	Very restrictive	Restrictive	—
Poland	Very restrictive	Restrictive	Liberal	Very restrictive	Very restrictive	—	Very liberal
Spain	Restrictive	Liberal	Liberal	Liberal	Liberal	Restrictive	Restrictive
Italy	Restrictive	Very restrictive	Liberal	Liberal	Liberal	Liberal	Restrictive
Turkey	Restrictive	Restrictive	Liberal	Very restrictive	Very restrictive	—	Very restrictive
Greece	Very restrictive	Very restrictive	Liberal	Very restrictive	Very restrictive	Very restrictive	—

1. The table provides a partial update of information that first appeared in Nicoletti (2001). The partial update is based on information provided by a number of Member countries on reforms undertaken since 1998. A complete update for all Member countries has not been done. The table summarises a number of detailed indicators which are set on a scale from 0 to 6 according to an increasing degree of restrictions to competition in each sector. Detailed information on regulatory conduct is then summarised by using statistical techniques that determine the appropriate weight for each of the indicators. Countries are then classified as "very liberal", "liberal", "restrictive" or "very restrictive" according to their distance from an OECD mean.
2. Long distance (international and trunk) only.
3. The indicators for the retail distribution and mobile telephony industries were partially estimated.
4. The indicator for the retail distribution industry was partially estimated.

Source: Nicoletti (2001).

Figure 4. **Product market liberalisation in OECD countries**

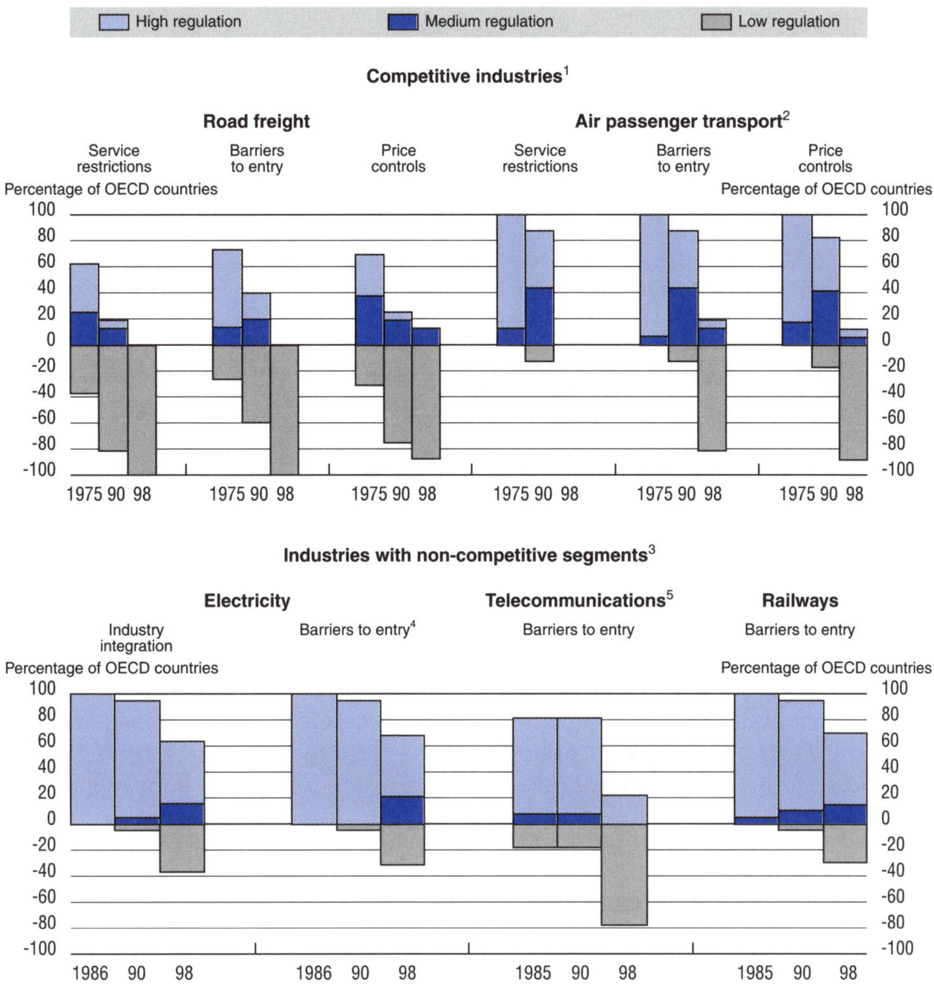

1. High regulation: Entry is restricted and prices or services are set or approved by a regulatory authority. Medium regulation: Some limited entry is allowed and businesses have some freedom to set prices or services. Low regulation: Businesses are free to enter and have full control over prices and the services they supply.
2. Domestic and regional routes.
3. High regulation indicates that access to competitive markets is restricted; for electricity, vertical integration. Medium regulation indicates that some limited market access is allowed; for electricity, limited vertical separation. Low regulation indicates that market access is free; for electricity, full vertical separation.
4. In electricity generation.
5. Fixed telephony: trunk and international.

Source: OECD (1992), *Regulatory Reform, Privatisation and Competition Policy*, OECD International Regulation Database.

Empirical studies point to a number of favourable economy-wide outcomes in those OECD countries where competition-enhancing regulatory reforms in service industries have gone further: *i)* the share of services in domestic output, employment growth and the catch-up in productivity growth have been higher; *ii)* distribution systems have been modernised; *iii)* rail and road freight transportation have become less costly; *iv)* air transport networks have been modernised and made more efficient, and airfares for all categories of travellers have declined substantially; and *v)* telecommunications and electricity supply have become more efficient and cheaper, especially for industrial consumers. Moreover, in many industries, regulatory reform has been matched by technical progress, innovation and product diversification. Furthermore, competitive pressures in liberalised markets have encouraged productivity-enhancing investment, particularly in information and communication technologies (ICT) (Nicoletti, 2001).

Recent cross-country analyses suggest a number of areas where a deepened commitment to regulatory reform and to liberalisation could contribute substantially to improving economic performance and raising living standards in the OECD area. Many of these are amenable to liberalisation of trade and investment, whether regionally or under the GATS. These include: *i)* the elimination of restrictive provisions concerning entry and/or investment in competitive service industries, such as retail distribution – for instance the removal of provisions discriminating against certain categories of service providers or investors (*e.g.* large outlets, foreign firms); *ii)* the opening up of international air travel routes to competition and the elimination of ownership restrictions regarding airline companies; *iii)* the creation of conditions for competitive provision of rail freight services; *iv)* a deepening of liberalisation in telecommunications, particularly as regards conditions for opening up the local loop to competitive service suppliers; and *v)* the acceleration of reforms in the electricity supply industry (Nicoletti, 2001).

Who stands to gain from open services markets?

Benefits for consumers

Perhaps the most surprising aspect of the recent controversies surrounding trade in services is the short shrift that is given to the interests of consumers. There is nothing new in the fact that consumers themselves are not vocal; the "public good" problem has always acted to reduce the involvement of end users in discussions of trade policy and tended to impart a producer bias to rule-making. This is arguably less true for services than for goods trade, as evidenced by the powerful influence exerted on telecommunications liberalisation during the course of the Uruguay Round by a number of user industries, most notably the financial service sector. Still, like manufacturing or agriculture, the service sector is not immune from the tendency to ignore or downplay consumer interests or to dress up self-serving proposals as pro-consumer arguments. Analyses that emphasise the interests and positions of producers rather than consumers can easily be skewed. In the services context, that means focusing on the interests of lawyers, doctors, health plan administrators, teachers, filmmakers, authors, public service employees and so forth, rather than those of clients, patients, students, moviegoers, readers and users of electric and water utilities.

The specific benefits that consumers enjoy as a result of liberalised trade in services are conceptually identical to the benefits from more open trade in goods. When markets are open to both domestic and foreign providers, consumers will ordinarily enjoy the results of price and quality competition.

Telecommunications offer the most prominent example of declining costs for both consumers and firms (see the special section following Chapter 3 for a more complete illustration of the benefits of liberalisation in a number of service sectors, including telecommunications). Figure 5 shows the vast reduction in the real costs of international telephone services, using as examples calls from the United States to Japan and the United Kingdom.

Figure 5. **Declining costs of international telephone calls, 1983-99**[1]

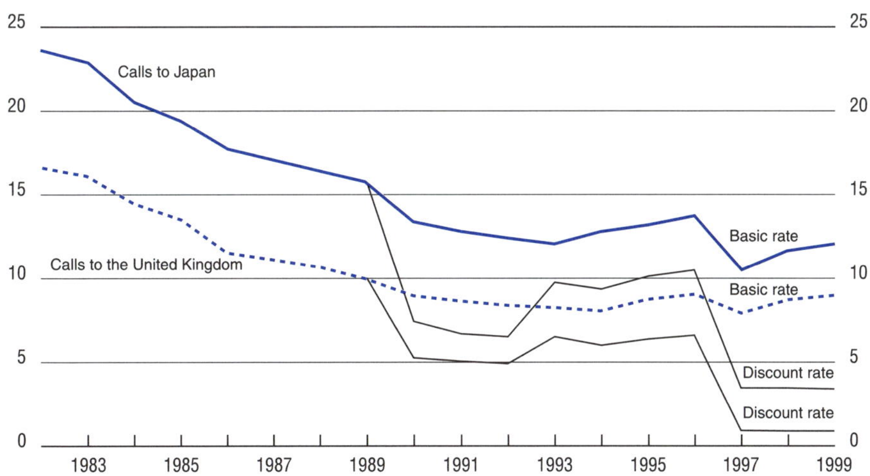

1. Rates charged by AT&T for residential customers in the United States making seven-minute calls at peak periods on 31 December, in constant 1999 USD.

Source: Calculated from Federal Communications Commission (1999).

In 1982, the real cost of placing a seven-minute call to Japan was USD 23.64 (in 1999 USD), but in 1999, a consumer using the cheapest AT&T rate paid just USD 3.36, an 85.8% reduction. The cost of a US-UK call fell by an astonishing 95% during the same period. The steepest reductions came in 1997, the year that the WTO successfully concluded the extended negotiations on market access for basic telecommunications services. In the 13 years from 1983 to 1996, the rates for calls to Japan and the United Kingdom dropped by 55.7% and 60.3%, respectively, but in just one year they dropped by another 67.3% and 86.8%. There can be little doubt that the GATS negotiations helped to consolidate and accelerate the price-cutting trend that was already under way in the United States and to spread it to other countries as well.

Increased competition in the telecommunications field brings more benefits than mere rate cuts, important though these may be. Telephone monopolies were once the most notoriously unresponsive service providers, with customers having to wait months, or (in some developing countries) years, for the installation of new lines. Through a combination of new technologies (especially cellular telephony) and new competition, telephone services are vastly improved today in most countries. The value of this development for businesses is incalculable and adds significantly to consumers' quality of life. The commercial and personal benefits are even greater when one considers the multiplier effect of the telephone as a gateway to the Internet.

Benefits for employees

Employees in the service sector generally enjoy higher pay and better working conditions than their counterparts elsewhere in the economy. Individual workers' bargaining power *vis-à-vis* employers, as well as their ability to find new employment when they change locations, are also enhanced by the interchangeable nature of many positions in the field, even if effects on collective bargaining are less clear. Several service industries are characterised by an above-average level of skills convergence among those who are proficient in the use of new technologies. An employee who is skilled in the requisite arts of one service sector, such as computer literacy and the manipulation of digitised data, may enjoy both upward and lateral mobility in the new economy. Portability of such skills across sectors is an important area for future research.

Figure 6 shows that, contrary to widely held public perceptions, employees in the service sectors tend to be better paid than workers in manufacturing. Calculated using International Labour Organization (ILO) data on salaried employees, the figure shows that workers in seven out of eleven service sectors earn higher wages than manufacturing employees, and that in all but one of the ten countries covered, the simple average wage across service sectors was higher than wages for

Figure 6. **Relative wage levels in service sectors**

Percentage difference with wages in manufacturing, selected countries and sectors

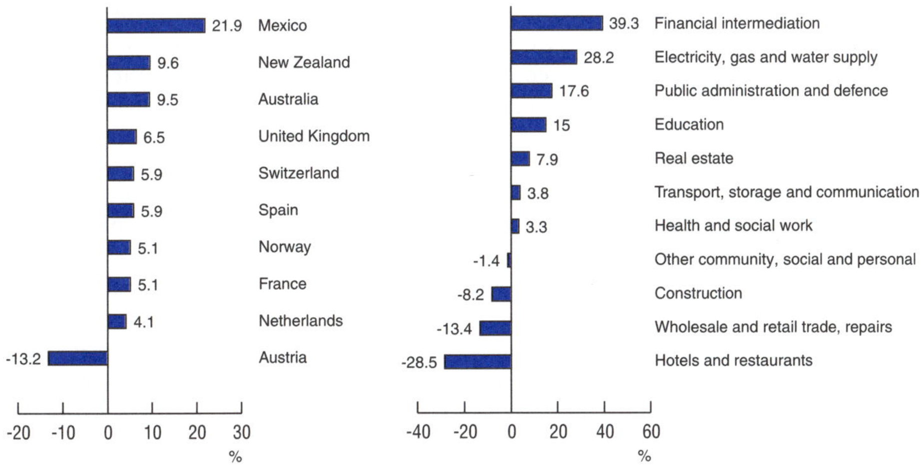

Source: Calculated from International Labour Organization data for 1998 or 1999 as available. Only countries for which sector-specific data were available are shown.

manufacturing. The wage premium is greater in those sectors that require more advanced education (*e.g.* finance, education) and/or tend to be staffed by unionised workers (*e.g.* utilities, public administration). Services, of course, are not universally better paid than manufacturing jobs, as can be seen by the relatively low pay in the sales and hospitality industries – both of which tend to be staffed by workers with less education or working on a part-time basis. Care must be taken to avoid generalisations based on these sectors – the infamous "hamburger flipper" characterisation of services employment. Such sectors, it should be noted, are often less exposed to international competition and are typically non-tradable as they require close proximity between sellers and consumers. As befits a sector that employs close to seven out of ten workers in OECD countries, the services economy generally has much more to offer prospective employees possessing higher levels of education and technical skills than the manufacturing sector, which may offer more beneficial employment for less skilled workers.

Benefits for firms

The most obvious beneficiaries of more open markets for services are those competitive, export-capable firms that hope to compete in overseas markets. Less apparent, but no less significant, are the benefits that extend to the firms that purchase these services. One of the key ingredients in the successful development of an industry, whether in the goods or service sectors, is the availability of business services that are affordable and of high quality. Countries that open their markets to competition from foreign providers – and become more efficient importers of these services – can reduce the costs and enhance the competitiveness of their producers across an array of goods- and services-producing industries.

The potential value of lower-priced services can be appreciated from the example of those services that are directly associated with trade in goods. Export-oriented producers of agricultural and manufactured goods depend on efficient transportation and affordable insurance for their overseas shipments. Improvements in the cost and quality of these services can contribute to the expansion of trade in goods. This is the clear implication of Figure 7, which shows the degree to which both tariffs and shipping costs for goods imported into the United States have declined in the past generation. As of 1975, tariffs and shipping costs amounted to USD 10.57 for every USD 100 worth of goods imported into the United States, but by 2000 the price of importing had dropped to USD 4.98. The reductions in shipping costs were responsible for USD 3.34 of the USD 5.59 savings (*i.e.* 59.7% of the total); lower tariffs accounted for the remaining

Figure 7. **Declining costs for importing goods into the United States**

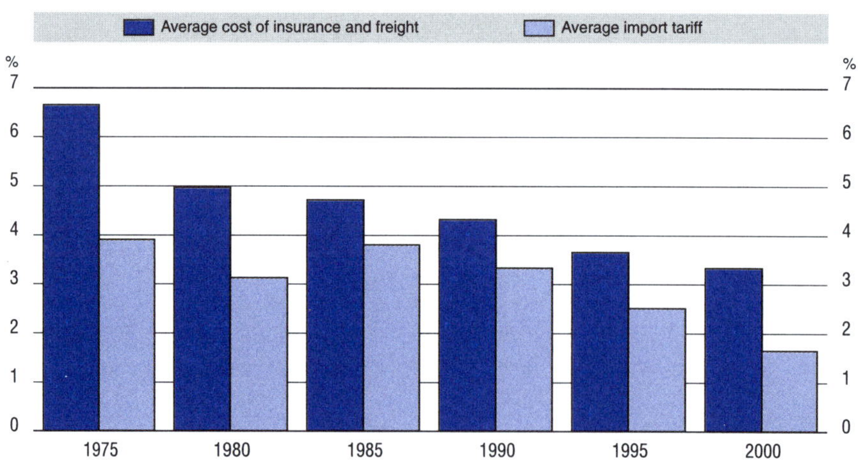

Note: The average cost of insurance and freight is calculated by comparing the CIF value of imports with the customs value. The 1980 calculation is based on FAS value rather than customs value.
Source: Calculated from US Department of Commerce data.

USD 2.25. In 2000 average shipping costs (3.33%) were just over twice the average tariff rate (1.65%). This example usefully recalls that further liberalisation of services may, to the extent that it increases competition and reduces the costs of freight and insurance of the goods to which particular services are linked, significantly reduce the transactions costs involved in merchandise trade.

The same logic applies to business services, also known as producer services or intermediate services. This category includes such activities as managerial, information technology, back-office operations or consulting engineering. Because these specialised services are typically produced under conditions of increasing returns to scale, it is usually beyond the capacity of individual firms to provide them internally; they will instead tend to contract out with external providers.

The Benefits of Open Services Markets: Empirical Evidence

Aggregate gains from services liberalisation

- The global welfare effect of services liberalisation is deemed to be roughly of the same order of magnitude as that associated with full liberalisation of barriers to trade in merchandise (agriculture and manufacturing). A study by Dee and Hanslow (1999) finds that the world as a whole is projected to be better off by more than USD 260 billion annually as a result of eliminating all post-Uruguay Round trade barriers. About USD 50 billion of this would come from liberalisation of agricultural trade, and a further USD 80 billion from liberalisation of trade in manufactures. The additional USD 130 billion – that is, half of the overall welfare gain – would come from liberalising services trade.
- Developing countries stand to gain relatively more than industrial countries from liberalising their services trade. The gains in welfare (expressed as a percentage of GDP) from a "hypothetical" 25% reduction of a vector of service sector protection were estimated to represent 1.2% for the United States and Japan and 1.0% for the EU. The corresponding values were 3.0% for the rest of South Asia, 2.9% for ASEAN countries, 2.5% for a group of newly industrialising economies, and 1.4% for India. The additional gains for OECD countries are relatively higher under services trade liberalisation than under goods trade liberalisation (Chadha, 1999).

Evidence of the economy-wide effects of services

- Following an increase in their own output, services have the capacity to generate demand for goods and services in other sectors. A study conducted for the World Bank (Azad, 1999) finds that for a unit increase in the output of electricity, gas, transport, public administration and health in Bangladesh, additional demand created for the output of other sectors ranges between 30% and 43%. Housing, construction and banking and insurance services spur demand for other sectors' output to the tune of 15-20% for a unit increase in their own output.
- For Bangladesh, Azad also finds that energy services (electricity and gas), banking and insurance as well as transport services are critically important inputs in the production of other sectors' output. In addition, services contribute between 20% and 25% to the production of the ready-made garments industry, the largest earner of foreign exchange for Bangladesh. The importance of services as inputs for other sectors' output implies not only that their availability is essential for production in other sectors of the economy but also that a cheap and better supply of services will substantially reduce the production costs of goods for which they are used as inputs.

- Another example concerns Chile's strong development of exports of foodstuffs, especially fresh fruit and fish. A reduction in flag discrimination in shipping led Chilean exporters to move away from domestic shipping lines and thus to ship their products at significantly lower cost. Many Chilean shipping lines shifted to flags of convenience and invested in equipment with the appropriate refrigeration technology. As a result, most lines were able to adapt to the changed environment (Hoekman and Mattoo, 1999).
- A major benefit of liberalisation is likely to be access to a wider variety of services that necessitate economies of scale. Consumers should derive direct benefits from diversity in services such as restaurants and entertainment, but also indirect benefits because a wider variety of more specialised producer services, such as telecommunications and finance, should lower the costs of producing both goods and services (Copeland, 2001). Countries with smaller markets are thus likely to have a strong interest in liberalising trade in producer services, since this can offset some of the incentives that firms have to locate in countries with larger markets (Markusen, 1989).
- An important defining characteristic of many services is that they may be costly to trade across borders (under modes 1 and 2 of the GATS). Hence, if foreign providers are to enter a market they will do so most efficiently through investment or, in GATS terms, commercial presence (mode 3). Markusen *et al.* (1999) developed a model to examine the benefits of a liberalised investment regime for intermediate services on a domestic economy even when the foreign provider "imports" from its home country much of the services that it supplies and economises on labour in the host country. Their results showed that: *i)* liberalisation of restraints on inward FDI in the service sector has a very powerful positive impact on the income and welfare of the FDI importing country, an impact that is much stronger than in traditional competitive models of goods trade; *ii)* the increase in the variety of imported services leads to increased total factor productivity in downstream industries; and *iii)* policies that aim to protect domestic skilled labour against competition from imported services can have the perverse effect of lowering the returns to domestic skilled labour. While the first two points are directly analogous to trade and investment in goods, the third point merits special attention. The model finds that even when foreign providers are engaged to supply services, the positive productivity and scale effects on downstream industry can be powerful enough to lead to an increase in the real wage of skilled labour after liberalisation. This implies that protecting a domestic service sector from foreign competition under mode 3 could have adverse impacts not only on the industries that consume those services but also on service professionals themselves.
- One of the most immediate results of service sector reforms, reported in many empirical studies, may be a fall in the profitability of incumbent firms. Declining profits at early stages of reform could in fact be viewed as a natural corollary of an adjustment process leading to more efficient production and marketing systems. Where internal reform efforts have foundered, for example due to cost rigidities or poor strategic management (for instance, a failed airline alliance), new entities have in many countries tended to emerge from take-overs, mergers or new business set-ups (WTO, 1998*a*).

Sectoral studies

Telecommunications

- Key indicators for the telecommunications sector confirm the significant role played by the Agreement on Basic Telecommunications (ABT) in the opening of markets for telecommunications services. The example of mobile telephony is a case in point. Global revenue from this sector reached USD 192 billion in 1999 and USD 230 billion in 2000, an increase of 25%. There were 650 million mobile cellular subscribers world-wide in 2000, compared with 214 million in 1997, a number the ITU predicts will grow to 1 billion by 2005 (ITU, 2000*b*).
- A recent OECD study revealed another dimension of the overall picture of mobile telephony by documenting the differentials in output growth and prices between liberalised and highly regulated countries over the 1990s (OECD, 2000*a*). In liberalised markets, the density of mobile phones grew much faster and prices fell more rapidly. The principal conclusions of the study (for the OECD area) were that productivity (defined as cellular subscribers per industry employee) generally increases with liberalisation, even before markets are actually liberalised, but average prices decline only once pro-competitive legal frameworks are in place (Nicoletti, 2001).
- In 1994, Chile introduced competition into its domestic and international telecommunications sector. This resulted in rapid modernisation of its infrastructure, new services and prices that are among the world's lowest. Prices for local telephone calls dropped by 36% between 1989 and 1994, 38% for long-distance calls and 50% for international calls (Wellenius, 2000). Similarly, in El Salvador, the telecommunications sector infrastructure was upgraded and service quality improved as a result of the 1998 sale of a majority stake in the country's public telecommunications operator and the auction of a second cellular license, in conjunction with the introduction of competition. The entire country is now covered for cellular service, and the delay for connection of a fixed line has been reduced from up to six *years* to just a couple of days (Mann, 2000).
- The results of reforms in the Philippines telecommunications sector have been unambiguously positive: the number of telephone lines has risen from just over 1 million before the introduction of the new programme in 1993 to 6.5 million by the first half of 1998. Cellular telephony has grown rapidly as well and the spread of telephone services throughout the country has improved. The proportion of municipalities served by telephones has increased from 20% to 37% since 1992; the number of participants, including many local-international partnerships, has increased significantly (APEC, 1998*a*).
- In Bermuda, pro-competitive regulatory reform, combined with infrastructure upgrading and increased FDI, has resulted in a decline of 66% in the cost of international telephone calls in the last four years.[1]
- The Internet is making contact within Africa and between Africa and the rest of the world significantly more affordable. E-mailing a 40-page document from Madagascar to Côte d'Ivoire costs USD 0.20, faxing it about USD 45, and sending it by courier USD 75. More and more African newspapers now post on-line editions, using foreign news found on the Internet.[2]

Financial services

- Liberalisation of trade and investment in the financial service sector can boost income and growth. A study of deregulation of US intrastate branching, *i.e.* where states relaxed restrictions on intrastate bank branching by allowing bank holding companies to consolidate bank subsidiaries into branching and permitted banks to open branches anywhere within state borders, found that this would stimulate growth by 0.3-0.9% of GDP for the ten-year period following deregulation and 0.2-0.3% thereafter (Jayarante and Strahan, 1996).
- In Chile, reforms of the financial sector resulted in a robust banking system in which suppliers and consumers operate with greater confidence. Bank deposits grew from USD 350 million in 1989 to USD 12.2 billion at the end of 1997; loans per employee rose from USD 27 000 to USD 490 000 and real interest rates decreased from over 40% to approximately 9% during the same period. Benefits to society as a whole include improved banking services, enhanced access to loans, more efficient channelling of funds into productive economic activities, such as agriculture and livestock, previously considered too risky. Those two sectors taken together, for example, received loans of only USD 54 million in 1990. In 1997, they obtained loans totalling USD 440 million (APEC, 1998*b*).
- Market expansion in all financial services has expanded employment in South Africa significantly. In addition, foreign entrants across all segments of the market have played an important part in making the country a regional financial centre. This has happened partly by using South Africa as a regional base, but also because their entry has improved the competitiveness of the financial services market by cutting prices, expanding the range of products and improving service (Hodge, 1998).
- Mauritius undertook regulatory, legislative and fiscal reforms in the areas of investment funds, investment holding and international trade to support the development of its offshore financial sector. This resulted in a significant increase in the total number of approved offshore entities in 1998 and generated total direct and indirect benefits of approximately 2.5% of GDP. In 1997, its double taxation agreement with India, combined with the gradual liberalisation of the Indian economy, generated estimated investment in India, through Mauritius, of USD 6 billion, or 32% of India's total FDI inflows and foreign portfolio investment in that year (UNCTAD, 1999*a*).
- Korea's financial liberalisation has addressed a number of financial vulnerabilities and strengthened the overall competitiveness of its financial sector. In the banking sector, foreign equity participation in existing domestic banks has helped to raise Korea's external credibility. The inflow of foreign capital increased demand in the securities markets, thus making it easier for corporations to raise long-term financing, improve their financial structures and increase profitability. Thus, liberalisation of the capital market contributed to economic recovery in the wake of the 1997 Asian financial crisis.[3]
- A study conducted for the World Bank and the WTO shows evidence of benefits from increased entry of both domestic and foreign banks into the Colombian banking system (Barajas *et al.*, 2000). The study shows that, after 1990, competition increased as a result of the *announcement* of the opening of new markets to new

entrants and that interest spreads decreased and loan quality (*i.e.* the share of non-performing loans in banks' balance sheets) improved as a result of improvements in banking regulation and supervision.

Transport services

- The average price of airfares in the United States, the first country to engage in far-reaching airline deregulation, has dropped from 0.144 USD per mile in 1970 to 0.079 USD per mile in 1997 (in 1982 dollars) (Hufbauer and Warren, 1999).
- Further liberalisation of international air transport services could offer large benefits. Removal in 1993 of bilateral restrictions on the free access to other EU markets for air transport services, price restrictions and slot allocations resulted in the issuing of nearly 800 new operating licenses, notably to small airlines. Thanks to lower and more flexible fares, demand for air transport has risen by about 20% (Commission of the European Communities, 1996*a*).
- In the two years following a bilateral "open skies" agreement between the United Kingdom and Ireland, economy-class fares between London and Dublin were almost halved, whereas flights between Dublin and other EU capitals remain much more expensive (Hufbauer and Findlay, 1996).
- The ongoing removal of bilateral quota restrictions on access to other EU countries, and the elimination of delays associated with border controls in the road transport sector, have so far cut the costs of border-crossing for haulers by 5-6% for a standard trip of 1 000 km (Commission of the European Communities, 1996*b*).
- In Australia, according to a study by the Productivity Commission (1998), the estimated reduction in prices resulting from the entry of another carrier into routes to and from Australia ranges from 2.4% to 7.7% for an increase in both Australian and foreign welfare. Airline profits fall and consumer surplus increases and the net gain is about AUD 30 million. Total net passenger movements increase by nearly 4% (in the second of the two years in which the simulation was run, and by 2% in the first year). The Commission also examined the effects of the introduction of an Open Club approach to aviation liberalisation. In their example, the club included Australia, China, Hong Kong (China) and Japan. The total benefits of openness accruing to club members was estimated at AUD 253 million in 1997.
- In Sri Lanka, privatisation, regulatory reform, upgrading of human resources as well as international co-operation in port services increased the importance of the transport sector in the economy. The net surplus generated by the country's air, shipping and port services has increased at an annual rate of 13% in recent years. Over the period 1979-97, container throughput grew nearly one hundred-fold (UNCTAD, 1999*b*).

Education services

- The overall contribution of international education to New Zealand's economy is estimated at USD 545 million, or some 0.5% of GDP. In comparison, the fishing industry accounts for 0.3% of GDP, oil and gas exploration for 0.7% and horticulture for 0.9%. Employment directly attributable to foreign student expenditure in the country is about 4 500 full-time positions. The economic flow-on effects raise this total to over 10 000 jobs (Infometrics Consulting, 2000).

- In the United States, the education sector is ranked fifth in terms of services export revenue, accounting for 4% of total services revenue in 1999 and over USD 14 billion of export receipts in 2000.[4] In Australia, approximately 150 000 foreign students attended the country's universities in 2000, and in 1999/2000, education services exports reached an estimated USD 3.2 billion.[5]
- In 1998, the United States hosted 32% of the foreign students within the OECD area, followed by the United Kingdom (16%), Germany (13%), France (11%) and Australia (8%) (OECD, 2000*b*).
- Education and competence in ICT is as important as technology in addressing digital divide problems. A recent OECD study showed that in the Netherlands in 1999, those with higher vocational or university-level education had significantly higher rates of access to both personal computers and the Internet than those with secondary education only (OECD, 2000*b*). Insufficient levels of education have been identified as one among several factors (others are age, race and geographical location) that can lead to technological marginalisation, even within countries with above average rates of Internet usage (Mann, 2000).

Notes

1. See Service Industries Trends 2001 at: *www.sitrends.com/facts/figure.asp*?FIGURE_ID=36
2. "Tapping into Africa", *The Economist*, 9 September 2000.
3. "Korea's Liberalisation of Financial Services – Experiences and Lessons", paper presented to the APEC GOS by the Ministry of Finance and Economy, Republic of Korea, 2000.
4. WTO, *International Trade Statistics* 1999; United States National Committee on International Trade in Education, *www.tradeineducation.org*
5. Australian Department of Foreign Affairs at: *www.dfat.gov.au*

References

APEC (1998*a*),
"The Impact of Liberalisation: Telecommunications Industry in the Philippines" (November), Singapore: APEC Secretariat, available at *www.apec.org*

APEC (1998*b*),
"The Impact of Liberalisation: Financial Service Sector in Peru" (November), Singapore: APEC Secretariat, available at *www.apec.org*

Azad, A. K. (1999),
"Inter-Industry Linkages of Services in the Bangladesh Economy (with a Case Study of the Ready-made Garments Industry) and Potential Services Trade", mimeo, Washington, DC: The World Bank.

Barajas, A., R. Steiner and N. Salazar (2000),
"Foreign Investment in Colombia's Financial Sector", in S. Claessens and M. Jansen (eds.), *The Internationalization of Financial Services: Issues and Lessons for Developing Countries*, London: Kluwer Law International, pp. 355-388.

Chadha, R. (1999),
"GATS and Developing Countries: A Case Study of India", mimeo, New Delhi: National Center for Advanced Economic Research.

Commission of the European Communities (1996*a*),
"The 1996 Single Market Review", Commission Staff Working Paper, Brussels: Commission of the European Communities.

Commission of the European Communities (1996*b*),
"Road Freight Transport", Single Market Review Series, Sub-series II – Impact on Services, Brussels: Commission of the European Communities, March.

Copeland, B. R. (2001),
"Benefits and Costs of Trade and Investment Liberalisation in Services: Implications from Trade Theory", paper prepared for the Department of Foreign Affairs and International Trade, Government of Canada.

Dee, P. and K. Hanslow (1999),
"Multilateral Liberalisation of Services Trade", Canberra: Australian Productivity Commission.

Hodge, J. (1998),
"Examining the Cost of Services Protection in a Developing Country: The Case of South Africa", paper prepared for the World Services Congress, Atlanta, November.

Hoekman, B. and A. Mattoo (1999)
"Services, Economic Development and the Next Round of Negotiations on Services", *Journal of International Development*, Vol. 12, pp. 283-296.

Hufbauer, G. C. and C. Findlay (eds.) (1996)
Flying High: Liberalizing Civil Aviation in the Asia Pacific, Washington, DC: Institute for International Economics.

Hufbauer, G. C. and T. Warren (1999),
"The Globalization of Services: What Has Happened? What Are the Implications?", mimeo, Washington, DC: Institute for International Economics.

Infometrics Consulting (2000),
"Economic Impact Analysis of Foreign fee-Paying Students", report prepared for the New Zealand International Education Marketing Network, Wellington.

International Telecommunication Union (2000*a*),
"Key Indicators for the World Telecommunication Service Sector", Geneva: International Telecommunication Union, available at *www/itu.int*

Jayarante, J. and P. E. Strahan (1996),
"The Finance-Growth Nexus: Evidence from Bank Branch Deregulation", in *Quarterly Journal of Economics*, No. 111, pp. 639-670.

Mann, C. (2000),
Global Electronic Commerce: A Policy Primer, Washington, DC: Institute for International Economics.

Markusen, J. R. (1989),
"Trade in Producer Services and in Other Specialized Intermediate Inputs", in *American Economic Review*, Vol. 79, pp. 85-95.

Markusen, J. R., T. Rutherford and D. Tarr (1999),
"Foreign Direct Investment in Services and the Domestic Market for Expertise", mimeo, Washington, DC: The World Bank.

Nicoletti, G. (2001),
"Regulation in Services: OECD Patterns and Economic Implications", Economics Department Working Papers No. 287, Paris: OECD, 8 February.

OECD (2000*a*),
Cellular Mobile Pricing Structures and Trends, Paris: OECD.

OECD (2000*b*),
Education at a Glance, Paris: OECD.

Productivity Commission (1998),
"International Air Services – Inquiry Report", Canberra: Productivity Commission, 11 September, available at *www.pc.gov.au/inquiry/airserv/finalrep/index.html*

UNCTAD (1999*a*),
"Assessment of Trade in Services of Developing Countries: Summary of Findings", a note by the UNCTAD Secretariat, UNCTAD/ITCD/TSB/7 (16 August), Geneva: United Nations Conference on Trade and Development.

UNCTAD (1999*b*),
"Analysis of Experiences in Selected Service Sectors", a note by the UNCTAD Secretariat, Geneva: United Nations Conference on Trade and Development.

Wellenius, B. (2000),
"Extending Telecommunications Service to Rural Areas – The Chilean Experience: Awarding Subsidies through Competitive Bidding", mimeo, Washington, DC: The World Bank.

World Trade Organization (1998*a*),
"Economic Effects of Services Liberalisation: Overview of Empirical Studies", background note by the Secretariat, S/C/W/26/Add.1 (29 May), Geneva: World Trade Organization.

Chapter 4

Acknowledging the Complexities of Services Reform

Pursuit of reform in services is no easy task, however, as there is often a need to balance the scope for promoting greater competition through new entry with the need for regulation to offset market failures. The gains from reform will be reduced and may not materialise at all if only a subset of the policies that restrict competition are addressed. Examples abound of reform attempts that did not give rise to the expected benefits because other measures remained in place that allowed firms to collude or to prevent the emergence of vigorous competition.

In addition to a comprehensive approach to reform that considers the broad set of all relevant policies, reform efforts must also take account of the legitimate role of government to intervene to offset market failures and to achieve non-economic objectives, such as the universal provision of education or health-care services. Care must however be taken to design regulatory reforms so that such objectives continue to be attained in an efficient manner. As noted earlier, the case for liberalisation of trade and investment needs to be distinguished from the need for regulation or regulatory reform. Regulation to achieve fiduciary, consumer protection, public health and safety objectives should be in place and strengthened where necessary, and be properly sequenced with liberalisation efforts. Such regulation, moreover, should apply equally to domestic and foreign service providers.

Strengthened multilateral disciplines on domestic regulations can play a significant role in promoting and consolidating domestic regulatory reform. Such disciplines can also equip developing country exporters with the means to address barriers to their own exports in foreign markets. For example, disciplines to deal with licensing and qualification requirements for professionals are necessary if market access commitments under mode 4 (temporary entry) are to have any value. One of the ironies of the GATS is that the provisions dealing with domestic regulation are among its weakest. This is largely a reflection of the learning-by-doing attributes of the first set of GATS negotiations and of the sheer novelty of the subject matter; Uruguay Round negotiators were essentially faced with a blank page. But it also reflects the difficulty of developing effective multilateral disciplines in this sectorally complex and diverse area without seeming to encroach upon national sovereignty and unduly limiting regulatory freedom.

Buyers of services are often inadequately informed about the characteristics of sellers, *e.g.* the competence of doctors and lawyers, the safety of transport services or the soundness of banks and insurance companies. Regulation can help offset such market failures but may also impede trade. For example, in the case of professional services, low standards and disparities in domestic training and examinations can become a major impediment to obtaining foreign recognition. Thus, inadequacies in domestic regulation can legitimise external barriers to trade. More important for many developing countries is the fact that inadequate domestic regulation may give rise to serious internal distortions. Thus, the need for effective regulation of financial services was highlighted by the recent experiences of a number of countries. It is clearly a necessary condition – many would in fact argue a pre-condition – for benefiting fully from liberalisation of trade and investment. Moreover, the absence of pro-competitive regulatory policies may substantially reduce the social payoff to privatisation if it merely results in transfers of rent from the public purse to the new private owners of the firms, be they domestic or foreign.

For service sector policies – and national commitments on trade and investment in services in the WTO or in regional trade agreements – to contribute to development, liberalisation will in most instances need to be conditional on *strengthened* regulation. Although attracting more FDI is often the best way to enhance competition in service industries, privatisation and take-overs of domestic firms may also give rise to excessive market power and monopolistic pricing. Regulation and competition policy may therefore need to be in place to complement liberalisation of trade and investment. Such institutions can be costly and may require sophisticated skills, and thus present challenges that are likely to be most acute in developing countries. For example, a recent study conducted at the World Bank noted that the total cost of government in the Caribbean island of Dominica was USD 41 million a year, while a bare-bones regulatory authority was likely to cost USD 2 million each year, or 5% of the budget (Hoekman, 2001). To some extent, such costs can be recovered through fees or regional co-operation, but for many developing countries external technical assistance will be needed to help ensure that adequate regulation and an ability to enforce it are in place.

Regulatory intervention will also typically be required to ensure that liberalisation improves access of the poor to essential services. For instance, competitive provision of subsidised public access helped to increase household ownership of a telephone in Chile from 16% in 1988 to 74% in 2000. Providing international assistance to meet the costs of the required subsidy programmes could greatly facilitate liberalisation by ensuring that the needs of the poor would be met.

Aside from the need for regulation to address market failures and secure key non-economic and social policy objectives, another important issue is the proper sequencing of internal regulatory reform and external opening. Several studies on financial sector reform have shown how premature liberalisation of capital flows, particularly in countries prone to experiencing macroeconomic instability, may compound exchange rate volatility and engender capital flight. By contrast, in countries with relatively stable macroeconomic performance and effective financial supervision, regulatory reform and trade liberalisation can readily work in tandem. Care must be taken, however, to avoid instances in which countries invoke regulatory inadequacies in order to postpone or unduly delay market opening, as the opportunity cost of foregoing reforms may be significant, particularly in key enabling industries. The challenge is to promote orderly adjustment, an objective the GATS is particularly well suited to support, by afford ing WTO members full freedom to choose the sectors and terms on which a progressive opening can be achieved.

Liberalisation of the service sector is not a panacea, however, and many of the benefits flowing from greater market openness may take time to materialise. In contrast, the costs associated with the rationalisation of service industries will appear early in the guise of changes in the structure of industry ownership and possibly displacement of labour. Opposition from affected workers, incumbent firms (domestic or foreign) and bureaucracies, which will often perceive liberalisation as a threat to employment, profitability or rent-seeking behaviour, add to the complexity of efforts to liberalise services. Such concerns help explain why some WTO members support the idea of embedding an emergency safeguard mechanism in the GATS, even as significant questions of operational feasibility remain unanswered in this area (Sauvé, 2001*a*; Gauthier *et al.*, 2000).[6]

As with trade in goods, liberalisation of trade and investment in services can expose countries to a potential loss of output and employment. However, it also exposes the domestic economy to greater levels of competition, a larger variety of technologies and products and a broader market for exploiting scale economies. These benefits to downstream users and final consumers may well offset any losses in the competing service sector.[7]

An important dimension of the liberalisation of trade and investment in services is that the adjustment associated with greater market openness is generally smoother in many service sectors than in some more traditional areas of goods production. This is so for three reasons, First, adjustment in service industries such as telecommunications and finance often occurs within a dynamic sectoral environment, where expanding market segments and firms can more readily absorb workers from shrinking sectors. Workers who face a greater risk of being negatively affected by such changes may find it easier to re-position themselves within a dynamic economy that generates favourable income and employment opportunities than in a stagnant system that defies or resists change (Adlung, 2000). Second, most international trade – some four-fifths of it – continues to take place in manufactured products. This generally lessens the direct exposure of service sector workers to trade-related job displacement. Third, and perhaps most importantly, owing to a lower degree of sector-specific professional specialisation and above-average educational levels, service sector employees in many fields tend to display greater overall labour market mobility. This characteristic may explain the observed tendency for displaced workers in non-manufacturing activities to experience shorter periods of unemployment, higher overall reemployment rates, and smaller earnings losses on average upon reemployment than workers in manufacturing.[8]

Research carried out by Lori Kletzer at the Institute for International Economics shows that import competition may be associated with low reemployment rates because vulnerable workers, those at risk of job loss as a result of rising competition from imports, experience difficulty gaining reemployment because of their individual characteristics. She concludes that it is not import competition *per se* that is at fault; the issue is who gets displaced from (and employed by) industries with rising import competition. Says Kletzer: "What limits the reemployment of import-competing displaced workers? The same characteristics that limit the reemployment of all displaced workers: low educational attainment, advancing age, high job tenure, minority status, marital status. Compared to high school dropouts, workers with a college degree (or higher) the great majority of whom are employed in service industries, are 25 percentage points more likely to be re-employed, high school graduates 9.4 percentage points more likely and workers with some college experience 11 percentage points more likely to be re-employed."

A recent study by Canada's Department of Foreign Affairs and International Trade documents the country's broad-based shift towards a knowledge-based service economy and the higher returns this shift entails for workers with higher educational levels. The study confirms that services are, overall, more knowledge-intensive than other sectors, employing many more well-educated workers than any other sector of the Canadian economy. Service industries, moreover, have many of the best jobs in the economy. Such findings belie the notion that the employment shifts towards services represent a shift from "good" to "bad" jobs or signal a deterioration in Canadian living standards. The study concludes that expanding the services economy, in part through rules-based liberalisation of trade and investment, will likely help sustain and create higher-quality jobs for Canadian workers (Chen, 2001).

Adoption of pro-competitive regulatory reforms and liberalisation of trade and investment in services can be expected to help relieve some of the constraints weighing on developing countries' growth potential. Evidence shows that such effects are likely to be greatest with regard to establishment-related trade.

Foreign capital inflows provide a higher savings rate and thus the potential for a higher investment rate as domestic funds can be diverted to other opportunities. Inflows of foreign capital also lower the balance of payments constraint on growth and allow for lower real interest rates. This, and the boost to short-term growth rates, tend to crowd in greater domestic investment. As foreign entrants will employ significant numbers of locally hired workers, this process typically support the development of human capital and knowledge-based industries. Moreover, the average wage that workers in foreign affiliates command, in both developed and developing economies, typically is at a premium over wages in competing domestic industries (Graham, 2000).

Chapter 5

Globalisation and its Discontents: the GATS Critics

Critics of new GATS negotiations, who, as noted earlier, are mostly from the OECD area, assert that more open markets will bring about a myriad of undesirable outcomes. Most of their claims and concerns can be classified as follows:

- Liberalisation will reduce the availability, increase the costs, threaten the quality or skew the distribution of social services such as health and education or vital utilities such as electricity and water.
- Unlimited entry of cultural products such as films, television programmes and music will undermine, displace and marginalise indigenous cultures.
- Giant multinational corporations will be the only real beneficiaries of open services markets, and the GATS will give them the means to overwhelm both their smaller competitors, especially in developing countries, and the regulatory powers of national governments.

These myriad concerns are often lumped together under the umbrella term "globalisation". This process is characterised in some quarters as "a new economic model [that] establishes supranational limitations on any nation's legal and practical ability to subordinate commercial activity to the nation's goals" (Nader and Wallach, 1996) or even as a conspiracy in which "the cultural patterns that still imbue most Third World cultures and that commit them to their largely self-sufficient lifestyles must be ruthlessly destroyed and supplanted by the culture and values of Western mass-consumer society" (Goldsmith, 1996).

Clearly, globalisation has different implications for different people.[9] French Prime Minister Lionel Jospin recently expressed a more balanced view, noting that: "Globalisation encourages world growth but involves growing inequalities. It encourages the discovery of human diversity but carries with it the risk of standardisation. It frees up energies but brings in its wake negative forces that we need to be able to master.... The non-governmental associations and organisations do not have anything like the sovereign legitimacy or ability to act, especially when this legitimacy is founded in democratic elections. The role of states therefore remains determinant... If we know how to manage globalisation well, it can be a new stage in the progress of civilisation... Globalisation is an opportunity that we must seize, a promising reality that we must know how to craft so that it benefits humanity in its entirety."[10]

Although the term defies easy definition, globalisation implies two related but distinct processes. One is technological modernisation, the process by which new developments facilitate and accelerate the cross-border movement of goods and services. The rapid advances in telecommunications and related technologies are now doing for services what the development of safe and efficient transport did in the past for goods. Services that were once supplied exclusively by national providers can now be sourced almost anywhere that people have access to modern communications. Simply put, this aspect of globalisation means that "a company no longer needs to go abroad to be abroad" (Naim, 2001).

Where the first aspect of globalisation is essentially a change in degree – trade across borders is a longer-distance version of domestic sales – the second represents a change in kind. Globalisation also entails the commercialisation of some activities that had previously been insulated from the market. Nearly all goods have long been thought of as tradable commodities, but certain service sectors involve matters that were not previously considered "economic" in the traditional sense of the term. Teachers, doctors and professionals in other service sectors often consider their chosen callings to lie outside the commercial sphere and may resent the notion that the services they provide should be subject to the same market forces as, for example, automobiles or clothing. Those responsible for regulating such activities at national or global level typically share such sentiments. Education, health care and other "products" of the social service sector are often portrayed as fundamental human rights that should either be provided by the state or subject to regulation, rather than as commodities that should be rationed by the forces of supply and demand. Similar claims are made with respect to cultural goods and services, essential utilities and other sectors that are (or should be, in whole or in part) freed from the price mechanism and the profit motive.

It is this latter aspect of globalisation that seems to have inspired much of the recent backlash against further liberalisation of trade and investment in services. What seems at issue for many critics is not so much the transnational character of trade in services, but the question of whether these exchanges should be conducted on a market basis in the first place. Those who oppose the liberalisation of specific services often employ the same language when expressing their concerns. Whenever a group is against the inclusion of something new within the scope of market disciplines, it will urge that the item not be treated as a commodity. "Water is a basic human right", according to an official of the Canadian Union of Public Employees (CUPE), "not a commodity to be bought, sold and traded".[11]

Critics also point out that a "country's cultural heritage is not a mere commercial product" (Bishop, 1996); they bemoan the fact that "major newspapers around the world now report on education as a commodity" (Van Leeuwen, 2000); while others note that "information's epiphenomenal character is fundamentally inconsistent with commodity treatment" (Babe, 1996). Critics fear that bringing the more politically sensitive service sectors within the ambit of international trade rules will mean reducing the extent to which the production and allocation of selected services can be controlled by means other than market forces.

To a significant degree, such concerns underlie the current campaign directed against the GATS, which has been characterised as threatening the "democratic" provision of essential services. One author portrayed the GATS as an agreement "designed to facilitate international business by constraining democratic governance" (Sinclair, 2000). A more expansive example of this argument comes from a joint paper issued by Education International and Public Services International, which associated the GATS negotiations with a "democratic deficit" that "is progressively deepening as what effectively amounts to a covert world government is built step by step on the basis of the economic, financial and business interests of a handful of large corporations" (Education International, 2000).

The current debate over services is therefore more complex than the traditional antagonism between free traders and protectionists over trade in goods. In an "old GATT" dispute, the two sides would disagree sharply over the extent to which imports should be permitted access to the domestic market, but in the end they typically had one thing in common: both the supporters and the opponents of trade protection tended to be profit-oriented firms. Consumers of the goods in question might theoretically join in the debate, but in actual practice the "public good" problem – the fact that benefits of liberalisation will likely be thinly spread over the entire population whereas the costs are both more immediate and concentrated in certain sectors or categories of workers – almost always limits their effective participation as liberalisation advocates (Olson, 1965).

Public policy debates over trade in services attract a wider set of constituencies. In addition to profit-oriented firms and their employees, the participants in such debates may include those who purport to speak for consumers and recipients of public services, as well as an array of service providers and civil society groups concerned with matters of consumer welfare, the environment, human rights or development issues. The spectrum of services providers typically ranges from pure public monopolies to traditional firms, with a variety of hybrids (such as partial public ownership, regulated monopolies and non-profit organisations) also playing a role. Public-sector employees and those of heavily regulated enterprises are particularly active, and rank in some countries among the sharpest critics of liberalised trade or investment in services. Some of their criticisms appear to be directed not so much at GATS or the WTO *per se*, but instead are warnings to national governments that the terms of the domestic social contract must be negotiated at home and not in supranational settings.

De *facto* liberalisation

Concerns over the supposed power of the WTO must be seen in a context where global services trade has already undergone significant, if largely spontaneous or *de facto*, liberalisation through two other mechanisms. These are the autonomous actions of national governments to remove regulatory restrictions and restraints on trade and foreign investment and technological advances that facilitate trade in areas previously thought to be non-tradable. The GATS 2000 negotiations may be seen in part as an exercise in codification that seeks to catch up with the current level of openness afforded by these changes.

Despite the fact that investment is not covered by a comprehensive body of multilateral disciplines governing its protection or liberalisation, it remains the driving force of deepening integration in the world economy (Sauvé and Wilkie, 2000). It remains, as well, the most powerful means of supplying services internationally, accounting for nearly seven of every ten USD of cross-border investment activity today. Figure 8 indicates the extent to which autonomous liberalisation of national investment regimes, both for services and for goods, was a hallmark of the last decade of the 20th century. In any given year, as many as half of the sovereign states made changes in their investment regimes. The overwhelming bulk of these changes was in the direction of greater market opening, rather than the

Figure 8. **A decade of *de facto* liberalisation: investment regimes in the 1990s**
Number and variety of changes introduced by countries in their investment regimes

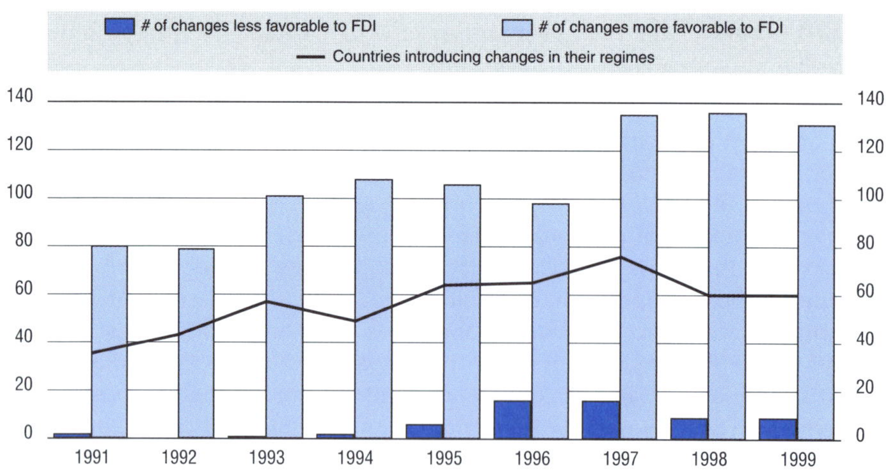

Source: United Nations Conference on Trade and Development (2000).

imposition of new or stricter limits on FDI. Even at the lowest point in the decade (1996), the observed trend was still "six steps forward for every backward step".

To the extent that they concern the supply of services through an established presence (so-called mode 3 of GATS on commercial presence), many of these liberalising initiatives have not yet been reflected in the schedules of commitments which countries negotiate in the GATS. An analogy can be drawn here between the applied and bound tariffs that govern imports of goods. Just as many countries apply tariffs that are well below their bindings, so too the statutory and regulatory practices of many countries in respect of services trade or investment are significantly more liberal than their bound obligations under the GATS. Prospective investors, whether national or foreign, know that a market-opening initiative which a country takes on its own initiative (but does not bind contractually) may subsequently be rescinded. When such commitments are bound in a trade agreement, however, the initiative becomes a firmer commitment that is less readily undone.[12]

There can indeed be no certainty that the wave of unilateral liberalisation observed in recent years, and especially since the entry into force of the GATS, which coincided with a period of sustained economic activity in many markets, can forever be assured or taken for granted. Moreover, despite the high potential benefits of competition and inward investment that flow from autonomous liberalisation, many governments, particularly of larger countries, may find it difficult for political reasons to liberalise autonomously. Hence the need to be able to point to matching liberalisation commitments – "concessions" in trade speak – by trading partners. Moreover, there is little doubt that governments of both developed and developing countries share an interest in ensuring that current popular misconceptions about the alleged effects of the liberalisation of trade and investment in services do not gain widespread currency or become self-fulfilling prophecies that could bring the process of virtuous, unilateral liberalisation to a premature halt.

Technology is another key ingredient of *de facto* liberalisation. The development of electronic commerce (e-commerce) is already exerting far-reaching influences on the globalisation of many service sectors. The Internet and other electronic means of transmission are large and growing avenues for the delivery of services. The first generation of GATS negotiators could not fully anticipate the emergence of e-commerce, which was not yet a commercial reality when the curtain fell on the Uruguay Round. Some analysts have argued that the Internet may already be making the GATS outmoded and that even in the absence of new trade agreements, advances in technology could still create further market openness in respect of services trade. It must be noted, however, that negotiations and technological developments are hardly wholly independent of one another. The principal *demandeurs* in the current set of negotiations are basing their plans in large measure on the expectation that those technological developments will offer even greater opportunities for expanding services exports.

Chapter 6

What the GATS Is – and Is Not

The conclusion of the GATS, which brought services trade into the multilateral framework of trading rules, was one of the most significant achievements of the Uruguay Round. The GATS offers for services trade the same stability that arises from mutually agreed rules, binding market access and non-discriminatory commitments that the GATT has provided for goods trade over the last five and a half decades. However, liberalisation of services trade is quite different from trade in goods, given the characteristics of services and the highly developed regulatory frameworks in place in many service industries.

The primary goal of the Uruguay Round in the services field was to put in place the GATS framework, through which liberalisation would be achieved on a progressive basis in successive negotiating rounds. Little real liberalisation – understood as implying a rolling back of existing discriminatory measures or measures impeding market access – was locked in (*i.e.* made legally binding) in the first negotiating round. Most members made commitments that bound the statutory and regulatory *status quo* (in some cases significantly less) and the sectoral coverage is quite limited in many members' schedules. An indication of the work that lies ahead for securing more meaningful market access commitments may be gleaned from a calculation of the share of commitments where no restrictions are maintained on market access and national treatment. For high-income countries, the share is about 25% of all services; for other members, it is less than 10% (Hoekman and Mattoo, 1999).

How the GATS operates

As a framework agreement that features several of the fundamental principles of the GATT – national treatment, most-favoured nation (MFN) treatment, transparency in domestic regulation, fair application of laws – the GATS covers, in principle, international trade in all services except those supplied in the exercise of governmental authority and, in the air transport sector, traffic rights and all services directly related to the exercise of such rights.

The GATS consists of three core components. The first is a framework of rules that lays out the general obligations governing trade in services, much as the GATT does for trade in goods. It provides for disciplines on transparency (of considerable importance given the regulatory density of services trade), MFN treatment, market access and national treatment. The framework is still incomplete, and rule-making efforts on certain issues, such as emergency safeguards, subsidies, government procurement and domestic regulation, are still under way. Second, the GATS includes annexes on specific service sectors (air transport, financial services, maritime transport and telecommunications) as well as the movement of natural persons. The third element consists of the schedules of commitments detailing the liberalisation undertakings of each WTO member.

The preamble to the Agreement sets out the some of the key considerations that underlie its continued negotiation. These include:

- The belief that a multilateral framework of rules and principles that aim progressively to liberalise services trade will assist the growth of international trade in services and contribute to economic development worldwide.
- Acknowledgement that the liberalisation process must respect the needs and rights of governments to regulate in order to pursue national policy objectives.
- Acknowledgement that the integration of developing countries into the multilateral trading system must be facilitated by reinforcing the capacity, efficiency and competitiveness of their domestic service industries.[13]

Negotiations on the framework of the GATS resumed in January 2000 and negotiating guidelines and procedures were adopted by the WTO Services Council at the end of March 2001. Both in the run-up to the November 1999 Seattle Ministerial meeting and since then, the area of services has been among the least problematic areas of inter-governmental discussions in the trade field. Since negotiations resumed, more than 130 negotiating proposals have been submitted by some 50 WTO members on a wide range of issues and sectors. Such developments attest to the importance attached by a large number of countries, both developed and developing, to continued progressive liberalisation under the GATS.

Arguably the most important principles in the GATS are its provisions on MFN treatment, transparency, national treatment and market access. The GATS does not impose any market access or national treatment commitments on WTO members unless the member voluntarily chooses to list that service in its schedule. Unlike the Agreement's market access and national treatment principles, which apply only to scheduled activities, the MFN provision of the GATS is a general obligation. A country is thus obliged to extend MFN treatment to all members in respect of all sectors, unless an exemption from MFN is taken for specific measures governing particular services. The MFN obligation means that a country will treat the service suppliers of another member no less favourably than it does the service suppliers of any other member. WTO members were given a one-off opportunity to draw up lists of MFN exemptions in the Uruguay Round (a possibility also afforded to subsequent acceding members). Derogations from MFN commitments are in principle subject to a ten-year sunset clause, and are also subject to periodic review or re-negotiation every five years. While MFN treatment guarantees equal treatment for all suppliers, regardless of their nationality, it bears noting that such treatment does not require any degree of market openness. As such, it is not necessarily a liberalising discipline, merely one aimed at securing non-discriminatory negotiating outcomes.

Given the high degree of regulation of many service activities, effective access to markets can depend crucially on services suppliers gaining accurate knowledge of the laws and regulations in force in a prospective market. The need for predictability is considerable in services trade, and is reflected in the fact that disciplines on transparency, contained in Article III of the GATS, are one of the Agreement's core general obligations. That is, it applies to all services subject to GATS coverage, regardless of whether members have scheduled (*i.e.* undertaken legally bound) liberalisation commitments. Article III requires members to publish all relevant measures of general application that pertain to or affect the operation of the Agreement and to notify any changes in laws and regulations affecting sectors on which commitments have been made. The promotion of greater transparency has also been at the core of work done so far in developing disciplines on domestic regulation under Article VI of the GATS.

The GATS distinguishes between four "modes" through which services can be traded. As Table 2 shows, the four modes might be compared to the means by which goods are exchanged: exports (mode 1); movement of consumers (mode 2); FDI, called "commercial presence" (mode 3); and movement of service providers (mode 4). These four modes of supply allow countries to specify any restrictions that they wish to make on their voluntary (or "positive") commitments on market access and national treatment. For any given service in which a WTO member chooses to make a commitment, it can set limits sector by sector and mode by mode with regard to its market access and national treatment undertakings. In other words, over and above so-called "horizontal" restrictions that may be maintained across the board (*i.e.* to all sectors, as is often the case for limitations on foreign investment or the temporary entry of service suppliers), countries have eight separate opportunities to indicate how they will treat foreign service providers in any given sector (*i.e.* market access and national treatment restrictions can be lodged against each of the four modes of supply).

The two key liberalising principles of the GATS, which WTO members can subscribe to on a purely voluntary basis, are contained in Articles XVI and XVII of the

Table 2. **The four modes of supply for international trade in services**

	Definition	Examples (architecture)
Mode 1: Cross-border supply	The supply of a service "from the territory of one Member into the territory of any other Member". The service crosses the border, but both the provider and the consumer stay home.	A Swiss architectural firm designs a building to the specifications of a Mexican client and sends the blueprints to Mexico.
Mode 2: Consumption abroad	The supply of a service "in the territory of one Member to the service consumer of any other Member". The consumer physically travels to another country to obtain the service.	A Mexican client travels to Switzerland to engage the services of an architectural firm.
Mode 3: Commercial presence	The supply of a service "by a service supplier of one Member, through commercial presence in the territory of any other Member" (*i.e.* investment through the establishment of a branch, agency, or wholly-owned subsidiary).	A Swiss architectural firm establishes an office in Mexico to serve the local market.
Mode 4: Presence of natural persons	The supply of a service "by a service supplier of one Member, through presence of natural persons of a Member in the territory of any other Member". Private persons temporarily enter another country to provide services.	An individual Swiss architect travels to Mexico to work directly for clients.

Agreement, dealing respectively with market access and national treatment. Article XVI (Market Access) consists of six different types of limitations on market access which must be scheduled if WTO members wish to maintain them. Such limitations, the bulk of which relate to non-discriminatory measures of a quantitative nature, comprise certain measures that: *i)* limit the number of services suppliers; *ii)* limit the total value of services transactions or assets; *iii)* limit the total number of service operations or the total quantity of services output; *iv)* limit the total number of natural persons who may be employed in a particular service sector; as well as; *v)* restrict or require specific types of legal entity or joint venture through which services may be supplied; and *vi)* limit the participation of foreign capital.

Article XVII (National Treatment) also permits members to schedule and maintain limitations on non-discrimination. It is in this regard fundamentally different from the unqualified obligation of national treatment applicable to goods trade under the GATT. The distinction arises from the absence of tariff protection for services, which means that an unqualified market access and national treatment commitment would in many instances amount to fully free trade in services.

Exceptions and safeguards

Criticisms of the GATS are often based on the belief that the Agreement will eventually bring any and all service sectors within its liberalising scope and that these will be wholly and irretrievably "lost" to the regulatory protection of national governments. In fact, the Agreement establishes a series of opportunities for countries to limit, condition or even suspend the commitments that they make. The principal limits and instruments are summarised in Table 3, which compares the GATS rules on trade in services with their GATT counterparts on trade in goods. The exceptions for services are arguably broader than those established for goods trade.

Taken together, these rules offer the following options for a country that wishes to exclude a service sector from its GATS commitments, restrict their extent, justify a breach of those commitments or opt out of the multilateral trading system altogether:

- **It can simply decline to make any commitments.** Nothing in GATS compels member countries to bind or liberalise any specific sector, and a country may choose to keep a sector outside the scope of its commitments indefinitely. In this respect, the sectoral coverage of services subject to specific commitments under the GATS is much less complete than that of goods under the GATT. While the majority of GATT members have bound most or all of their goods tariffs, many have so far left a large number of their service sectors "unbound".

- **The country is free to qualify its commitments in any given sector or subsector.** For each of the four modes of supply covered by the GATS, a WTO member can either specify that it is "unbound" (*i.e.* the country has made no commitments in that sector for that mode of supply) or make a more specific reservation. For example, the country might retain existing discriminatory limitations on foreign investment or set limits on the number of suppliers, the total value of service transactions or assets, the total number of natural persons employed in a particular sector, etc. A WTO member can also bind less than the statutory and regulatory *status quo* or commit to future liberalisation, so that incumbent suppliers can prepare for new market conditions and the necessary regulatory regimes can be established.

- **The country may apply horizontal limitations to all services.** For example, many countries have listed horizontal limitations applicable to all sectors on the commitments for movement of persons or on those governing investment (commercial presence) in service activities. For instance, some WTO members maintain the right to review all inward FDI flows above a certain

Table 3. **Exceptions for goods and services in WTO agreements**

	Exceptions for goods under GATT 1994	Exceptions for services under GATS
Bindings	A country generally cannot apply a tariff rate that is higher than the binding to which it has agreed in GATT/WTO negotiations. There is no ceiling on the tariffs that can be applied on unbound items, however, and the country might agree to a bound rate that is significantly above the applied rate (thus leaving room to raise the applied rate if circumstances warrant such a move).	A country can exclude a sector from its GATS commitments either entirely (by leaving the sector out of its schedule of commitments) or partially (by specifying that it is "unbound" for one or more of the four modes of delivery, or otherwise setting limits on access).
Discrimination	GATT rules generally require that countries extend MFN treatment to all WTO members, and require national treatment on certain matters (*e.g.* sales taxes). The Agreement nevertheless allows countries to discriminate among trading partners via free trade agreements and customs unions, provided that the agreements meet certain requirements.	A country is free to discriminate against foreign providers *vis-à-vis* domestic providers in unbound sectors, or in committed sectors where it has specified a national treatment exemption. It can also discriminate between foreign providers in a sector if it takes an MFN exemption. GATS Article V (Economic Integration) also allows members to discriminate in favour of parties liberalising trade in services in economic integration agreements, subject to such agreements meeting Article V requirements on WTO compatibility.
General exceptions clause	GATT Article XX establishes a series of grounds on which countries can employ measures that restrict imports, provided that the measures are not "means of arbitrary or unjustifiable discrimination between countries where the same conditions prevail, or a disguised restriction on international trade". These include measures necessary to protect public morals; human, animal or plant life or health; national treasures; etc.	GATS Article XIV is generally similar to GATT Article XX, but does not provide for some exceptions (*e.g.* restrictions on gold movements) and includes others that are uniquely important to services (*e.g.* the protection of confidential records).
Safeguards	GATT Article XIX permits countries temporarily to suspend concessions or otherwise restrict imports when these imports cause substantial injury to domestic industries. Countries are no longer required to provide compensation to trading partners when invoking this "escape clause".	GATS Article X provides for multilateral negotiations on the question of emergency safeguard measures (counterpart to GATT Article XXVIII).
Modification of commitments	GATT Article XXVIII allows countries, at any time, and under special circumstances, to enter into negotiations to modify or withdraw a concession, subject to agreed compensatory adjustments with primarily concerned contracting parties.	GATS Article XXI allows countries to modify or withdraw a specific commitment anytime after three years; compensation must be provided to other countries whenever such action is taken.

Table 3. **Exceptions for goods and services in WTO agreements** (*cont.*)

	Exceptions for goods under GATT 1994	Exceptions for services under GATS
National security	GATT Article XXI allows countries to take otherwise GATT-illegal actions when the country considers such action to be necessary to safeguard its "essential security interests". In practice, countries have had broad discretion to invoke this provision.	GATS Article XIV bis is nearly identical to GATT Article XXI, except for the further requirement that members inform the Council for Trade in Services "to the fullest extent possible of measures taken under [this provision] and of their termination".

value threshold or to restrict temporary entry to certain types of service providers (*i.e.* highly skilled).

- **A country can invoke GATS Article XII (Restrictions to Safeguard the Balance of Payments)** provisions to suspend a commitment in the event that it is found to cause adverse effects on its balance of payments.
- **A country can invoke the various general exceptions in GATS Article XIV (General Exceptions)** to justify existing regulations, or to enact new ones, in pursuit of legitimate public policy concerns. Such exceptions can be invoked where necessary to protect major public interests, including safety, human, plant or animal life or health, national security or public morals. The exceptions foreseen under GATS Article XIV (General Exceptions) override all other provisions of the Agreement, allowing a WTO member to violate or withdraw its own commitments if necessary.
- **A country can ultimately withdraw from the GATS and the WTO altogether.** It bears recalling in this regard that no WTO member has to date done so and that countries have been queuing to join – rather than leave.

Chapter 7

Addressing Criticisms of the GATS

Many of the arguments invoked against the GATS reveal a misunderstanding of its purpose and operation. Unlike the GATT, the GATS is a new agreement, as yet incomplete. Concerns about the GATS, its effect on public services, its implications for national sovereignty and governments' ability to regulate are nonetheless genuine and need to be addressed. The new set of negotiations provides an important opportunity for governments to inform concerned constituencies about the GATS and how it affects national economic and social goals. This chapter addresses several of the most prominent misunderstandings arising in public policy debates about the GATS and the pursuit of rules-based liberalisation of trade and investment in services.

GATS and the right to regulate

The threat to a country's sovereign right to regulate, or the alleged transfer of regulatory authority from national governments to a supranational body such as the WTO, is a central plank of anti-GATS criticism. Agreements to accept a framework of rules, whether bilateral, plurilateral or multilateral, entail by definition some curtailment of sovereignty, although the decision to enter into such an agreement is itself an exercise of sovereignty. Through their membership in the WTO, over 140 governments have chosen to participate in a package of multilateral agreements because they recognise the overall net economic and social benefits that accrue from a rules-based trading system.

The progressive liberalisation – not deregulation – of services trade is the goal of the GATS, and of periodic negotiating rounds. A common error in the public policy debate over GATS is to use the terms "liberalisation" and "deregulation" interchangeably, as if they were synonyms. They are not, and it is simply wrong to assimilate regulation to trade restrictions. Services liberalisation, indeed, often necessitates regulation or re-regulation. But this is not to say that regulation, whether for economic or social purposes, cannot be designed, implemented or enforced in more transparent and efficient ways, with positive overall effects in terms of democratic governance.

The principal concern linked to loss of sovereignty is the consequent loss of a nation's freedom to regulate its service sectors in the manner it deems appropriate. Many service sectors are highly regulated in order to protect consumers, the environment and, in the financial service sector, to ensure a country's financial stability. Governments are understandably cautious when agreeing to subject themselves to common rules. Such precaution is reflected in the provisions of the GATS, which uphold the fundamental right of a government to regulate in order to pursue national policy objectives. The Agreement's preamble recognises, *inter alia*, "the right of Members to regulate, and to introduce new regulations, on the supply of services within their territories in order to meet national policy objectives".

It is certainly true that, as with any other legally bound undertaking in the WTO (or any other international treaty), the GATS can affect the regulatory conduct of member countries. Yet countries accept such disciplines because they deem them necessary for reaping the full benefits of international co-operation in a rules-based system. The GATS affords WTO members considerable flexibility in this regard. For those sectors, sub-sectors and modes of supply for which a WTO member agrees to schedule liberalisation commitments and has not included exceptions from the MFN treatment obligation, that country ultimately accepts, under the GATS, not to make its regulatory regime more restrictive in future (subject to trade concessions or retaliatory measures of commercially equivalent effect if a country decides, as it always can, to renege on its commitment). In scheduling commitments, WTO members may also opt, at their discretion, to treat foreign services and service providers in a non-discriminatory manner, *i.e.* to extend national treatment to the latter, now or in future. They can also decide, if they so desire, to eliminate, immediately or progressively, quantitative restrictions that impede access to their services markets.[14] Each of these decisions – like that of not scheduling commitments – remains the sovereign prerogative of WTO members.

Commitments under the GATS to grant market access in sectors where domestic regulation plays an especially important role do not entail any changes – and certainly no compromises – to regulatory standards or preferences. Those in force to protect the public, or to achieve universal access, *e.g.* in telecommunications or water supply, continue to apply regardless of the nationality of the supplier. Governments may also choose to impose additional requirements on foreign suppliers, something they typically do for instance in the case of professional licensing in medical services.

The specific obligations concerning domestic regulation in the GATS framework require members to regulate those service sectors in which they have made commitments in a reasonable, objective and impartial manner.[15] Article VI of the GATS (Domestic Regulation) aims to create more transparent domestic regulatory decision making, implementation and administration. The right of service suppliers to information on regulatory and administrative decisions and to judicial and administrative review and appeals processes is explicitly recognised. In both respects, the GATS champions principles of good governance.

The work programme foreseen under Article VI(4) of the GATS, on which discussions have continued since the end of the Uruguay Round, has provoked some of the strongest anti-GATS sentiment. Work in this area is designed to address the fact that non-transparent, unfair or unduly burdensome regulations at national level can potentially undermine the value of market access commitments freely entered into by a WTO member. Article VI(4) calls for the development of any necessary new disciplines to ensure that measures relating to qualification requirements and procedures, technical standards and licensing requirements do not constitute unnecessary trade barriers. No so-called "necessity test" has yet been developed under the Article VI(4) work programme. Discussions have proceeded slowly, reflecting the cautious attitude of governments in this area.

Disciplines relating to domestic regulation have however been developed specifically for the accountancy sector. These draft disciplines, which were adopted in December 1998 and are due to be integrated into the GATS at the conclusion of the current negotiations, would only apply to those countries that have made commitments on accountancy services. Critics have argued that the incorporation of such disciplines in the GATS could infringe upon governments' sovereign right to regulate by imposing a set of global standards on WTO members. However, the draft disciplines do not focus on the substantive content of qualifications in accountancy but seek to ensure procedural transparency in matters of licensing and qualification. The WTO is not a standards-making body, nor is it mandated to assess the content of national standards, be they technical or professional. The Article VI(4) work programme concerns itself with the *means* chosen by countries to pursue public policy objectives, and not the objectives *per se*.

The GATS and public services

A variety of claims are made according to which the GATS poses a threat to the provision of public services. It is said that it forces governments to privatise and allow competition in public services, that it obliges them to open them up to foreign trade and investment, and that it puts in danger the assurance of basic public services such as education, water distribution or health services. Indeed, one of the most contentious issues in the current debate over the GATS concerns the respective roles of the public and private sectors. It is sometimes argued that goods and services that are public in nature may be most efficiently and equitably provided (in whole or in part) by the public sector, often under monopoly conditions, or may be offered on a mixed public/private basis subject to stringent regulation.

The GATS does not dictate any specific role for the public and private sectors; countries are free to decide for themselves what sectors will be reserved for the state or state-owned enterprises. They remain entirely free to decide whether or not to open such sectors to outside competition and to make (or not) binding commitments in such sectors in their GATS schedules. It is misleading to suggest that the GATS forces governments to privatise or open up public services to competition, as the Agreement features no such obligations.

An important element in the debate over the GATS and public services is the fact that services supplied in the exercise of governmental authority are specifically excluded from the scope of the Agreement. Article I(3)(b) of GATS defines "services" to include "any service in any sector except services supplied in the exercise of governmental authority". This exception is defined in Article I(3)(c), which specifies that "a service supplied in the exercise of governmental authority" means "any service, which is supplied neither on a commercial basis, nor in competition with one or more service suppliers".[16] In effect, this provision carves out a potentially wide category of services from the scope of GATS rules.

The degree of government funding for public services varies widely across countries, depending on social and political preferences as to the role of the state in the provision of those services. The regulatory landscape in the education and health fields in most countries, developed and developing, is one in which public and private suppliers typically co-exist. The advantage of the GATS in this regard lies once more in its flexibility. It can accommodate a wide spectrum of positions with regard to services provided by the government and those supplied under competitive market conditions or by private entities on a not-for-profit basis.

Over and above the specific GATS carve-out for services supplied in the exercise of governmental authority, it is important to recall that the Agreement allows WTO members to:

- Regulate their service sectors in accordance with national policy objectives (subject to the limitations noted above in respect of areas where liberalisation commitments are undertaken). This is so regardless of the level of private sector involvement in a service activity. This key principle of GATS allows WTO members to guarantee that public policy objectives, such as universal service obligations, are achieved through an appropriate regulatory framework.
- Refrain from taking liberalisation commitments in any particular sector, subsector or mode of supply.
- Maintain or designate monopolies.
- Retain the ability to subsidise service activities in their territories (see below).

Assuming that a WTO member were to decide to open up one of its public service sectors to foreign suppliers, it remains free to select the activities or sub-sectors and to specify the conditions under which this can done. For instance, a decision to allow foreign services suppliers into the education or health sectors can apply to only a small number of selected sub-sectors, and remain subject to specific reservations carving out certain activities to particular categories of service suppliers. It bears noting that not a single country proposal to liberalise the provision of health services under the GATS has been formulated to date. Moreover, the three WTO members that have tabled negotiating proposals on trade in education services have all sought to clarify their circumscribed nature.[17] These proposals generally seek non-discriminatory treatment for those who provide education and training services on a *commercial* basis and meet the regulatory requirements of the host country. The United States, which submitted one of the proposals, has noted that it explicitly *does not* cover primary and secondary education and that a country's subsidies for higher education should not be made equally available to foreign providers (WTO, 2001*c*; Ascher, 2001). All proposals emphasise the central importance of preserving the ability of countries to apply regulatory measures necessary to achieve education policy objectives, including in respect of public funding.

The GATS and investment

As noted earlier, the GATS distinguishes between various "modes" of supplying services internationally. The third of the four GATS modes of supply refers to services supplied in a member country by a supplier from another member country via a commercial presence. This may take place, for example, through the establishment of a branch office or a subsidiary of the foreign company. Services trade via this mode often takes place in conjunction with the fourth mode – the presence of natural persons – given that directors, managers, specialists and other key personnel often need to be deployed abroad (at least initially) in order to manage a foreign operation.

Services trade through FDI is particularly important given the need for proximity between suppliers and consumers of services and the need to tailor service offerings to host market conditions. It is the area where by far the greatest number of liberalisation commitments were undertaken by WTO members in the Uruguay Round. This suggests the importance countries attach to reaping the positive benefits – high-paying jobs, human resource training, technology transfer, quality upgrading – typically associated with greater doses of FDI, while still retaining the freedom to regulate such activity. There is no denying that FDI raises many sensitive issues for host governments, in part because establishment involves foreign companies in a range of national rules and policy issues. Still, as Figure 8 reveals, the trend in host country FDI regimes has been strongly liberalising during the last decade. More often than not, such policy changes were enacted in a unilateral manner (Sauvé and Wilkie, 2000).

The argument is often heard that the GATS is principally an investment agreement, designed to promote the interests of large multinationals. While the GATS can be described as a multilateral agreement that covers FDI in the services trade context, it is not an agreement on investment *per se* and cannot be portrayed, as many GATS opponents have alleged, as a means of resurrecting the Multilateral Agreement on Investment (MAI). The GATS bears no resemblance to the MAI. This should come as no surprise, given that its provisions predate those of the latter and given the significant differences in membership between the OECD and the WTO.[18]

While WTO members may, via their GATS commitments, accord market access to foreign investors, they are not obliged to do so. In addition, governments are free, if they choose to make commitments on commercial presence, to maintain existing discriminatory or quantitative restrictions. The Agreement affords foreign investors no automatic right of establishment. The only obligations of WTO members are to schedule any existing restrictive measures they wish to maintain in sectors where liberalisation commitments are voluntarily undertaken and to ensure freedom of payments and transfers relating to investments in such sectors.

Governments can use the GATS selectively to encourage investment in sectors of their choice, subject to the conditions they wish to impose or retain, including with respect to technology transfers and the employment of local workers. The Agreement also permits governments to maintain foreign ownership restrictions in sectors where they have made commitments. The GATS promotes greater predictability through the permanency of commitments, an important element in attracting investment for developing countries. The GATS, moreover, provides no direct access by foreign investors to the dispute settlement mechanism of the WTO.

The flexibility described above helps explain why the GATS tends to be viewed as the most development-friendly agreement brokered in the Uruguay Round, and why a large number of WTO members feel that the GATS offers the greatest scope for incrementally beefing up the WTO's treatment of investment. Two important considerations of a factual nature to bear in mind in this regard are that services make up close to 70% of global annual FDI flows and account for an even greater proportion of discriminatory measures affecting cross-border investment activity (Sauvé, 2001*b*).

The GATS, subsidies and public procurement

In this area, two allegations are often made by GATS' critics. One relates to the presumption that the Agreement forces WTO members to grant governmental subsidies, notably in the fields of public health and education or cultural industries, to all comers on a non-discriminatory basis. The other is that it obliges countries to open up public procurement markets, including at sub-national level. The areas of subsidies and government procurement are areas where WTO members agreed at the end of the Uruguay Round to pursue negotiations with a view to developing any necessary multilateral disciplines (Sauvé, 2001*a*). No such disciplines currently exist in the services area, nor has any firm deadline been set to complete ongoing discussions in either area.[19]

Critics of the GATS claim that future subsidy disciplines would impinge on the sovereign right to support fledgling domestic service industries and services supplied by government monopolies alike. This is a particularly sensitive issue because service industries that typically benefit from subsidies are those which many critics argue should remain outside the scope of multilateral trading rules (*e.g.* health, education, audio-visual, utilities). At present, in sectors where a WTO Member has made market access commitments under the GATS, it can maintain the ability to subsidise national service suppliers on a discriminatory basis by listing such limitations on national treatment in its schedule of commitments. It retains, moreover, full freedom to subsidise services activities in sectors in which it has not made commitments and which appear on its list of exemptions from MFN treatment.[20] Moreover, and more importantly in the context of anti-GATS arguments, it bears noting that regardless of the outcome of discussions on subsidy disciplines, the GATS has no implications for the funding or subsidy of services provided in the exercise of governmental authority, as these services lie outside the scope of the Agreement (see below).

Meanwhile, disciplines on public procurement, including for services and construction, continue to be governed by the WTO's Government Procurement Agreement (GPA), whose membership is currently limited to 27 signatories (mostly from OECD countries). Like the GATS, the GPA affords signatories full freedom to decide where and under what conditions to undertake market opening commitments for covered entities, including with regard to purchases by sub-national governments.

The GATS and dispute settlement

The WTO's Dispute Settlement Understanding (DSU) inspires some of the most extreme claims by opponents of trade liberalisation. Critics often portray the DSU as a tool by which countries' laws might be overturned. In fact, WTO members retain the sovereign right to establish their own laws. Neither the DSU nor any other international body has the authority to invalidate the laws of sovereign states. The most that the DSU can do, in the event that it finds a country's laws to be incompatible with its obligations under the GATS, is to give that country a choice among three alternatives. The preferred outcome is that the country brings its laws into compliance with the obligations that it has undertaken. Failing that, the country can either compensate its trading partners (*e.g.* by liberalising trade in some other area), or be subject to retaliation (of commercially equivalent effect) on the part of those countries whose interests have been injured. The retaliatory option is the least preferred outcome. It is also the least used in practice. In the absence of WTO rules, where "might" would likely supplant "right", retaliation would probably be the one most frequently employed by parties to a dispute, typically on a unilateral basis and to the benefit of the most economically or politically powerful countries.

The DSU does not operate under the often alleged principle that trade rules trump all other considerations. As with WTO rules governing trade in goods, the GATS establishes exceptions (in Article XIV) that extend special treatment to measures affecting national security, human, animal or plant life and health, public morals, governmental activity and other legitimate considerations of public policy (see Box 2). The Agreement also allows members to introduce restrictive measures in instances where liberalisation commitments may be shown to induce adverse effects on a country's balance of payments (in Article XII). The contention that a measure is justified by one or more of the above exceptions or restrictions remains, however, a refutable proposition that can be challenged by another WTO member and decided by a dispute settlement panel.

It bears recalling, moreover, that the GATS offers WTO members full freedom to limit their commitments or to exclude entire sectors from their liberalisation schedules. The DSU does not override such protections. Indeed, WTO members cannot be accused of breaching specific commitments they have not undertaken.

The GATS and developing countries

The claim is often made that the GATS, and the liberalisation of trade and investment in services, primarily serve the interests of large multinational firms and are thus almost inherently inimical to the growth and development prospects of the world's poorer countries. As will be pointed out in Chapter 8, the north-south tensions that characterised the early phases of negotiations on trade and investment in services are largely a thing of the past. There is, indeed, considerable evidence to suggest that developing countries are deliberately, if often autonomously, encouraging foreign competition in key sectors in order to upgrade their domestic services infrastructures. Moreover, and as Figures 2 and 3 make clear, developing countries are today major stakeholders in the GATS process. Developing countries are no longer merely importers of services, and their

Box 2. General exceptions for services as provided for in GATS Article XIV

"Subject to the requirement that such measures are not applied in a manner which would constitute a means of arbitrary or unjustifiable discrimination between countries where like conditions prevail, or a disguised restriction on trade in services, nothing in this Agreement shall be construed to prevent the adoption or enforcement by any Member of measures:

a) necessary to protect public morals or to maintain public order;

b) necessary to protect human, animal or plant life or health;

c) necessary to secure compliance with laws or regulations which are not inconsistent with the provisions of this Agreement including those relating to:

- *i*) the prevention of deceptive and fraudulent practices or to deal with the effects of a default on services contracts;
- *ii*) the protection of the privacy of individuals in relation to the processing and dissemination of personal data and the protection of confidentiality of individual records and accounts;
- *iii*) safety;

d) inconsistent with Article XVII, provided that the difference in treatment is aimed at ensuring the equitable or effective imposition or collection of direct taxes in respect of services or service suppliers of other Members;

e) inconsistent with Article II, provided that the difference in treatment is the result of an agreement on the avoidance of double taxation or provisions on the avoidance of double taxation in any other international agreement or arrangement by which the Member is bound."

increasing participation in services trade and the expansion of their service exports are central objectives of the GATS.

Apart from the general structure of the GATS and the flexibility, described throughout this study, that makes it possible to accommodate the interests of countries at different stages of development, a number of GATS provisions deal specifically with the particular situation of developing countries. Article IV (Increasing Participation of Developing Countries) provides that increasing the participation of developing countries in world trade should be facilitated through specific commitments, notably relating to: *i*) the strengthening of domestic services capacity; *ii*) the improvement in their access to distribution channels and information networks; and *iii*) the liberalisation of market access in sectors and modes of supply of particular export interest. Article IV also provides for the establishment of contact points in developed country members and others where possible, with the objective of facilitating the access of developing countries to information. Other general provisions in the Agreement include special conditions that take into account the specific needs of developing countries.[21]

Chapter 8

Negotiating Challenges Under the GATS

Governments at all levels of development today recognise the vital role played by an efficient and vibrant service industry in the process of economic and social development. Unilateral (autonomous) reform efforts are being undertaken by many countries. The issue is how to fit these into the GATS, how to use the GATS to push domestic reform efforts forward, how to respond to pressures from other countries that desire greater access to domestic markets and what to ask in return.

Multilateral liberalisation of services trade is generally more difficult than that of merchandise trade, as some of the defining characteristics of services trade, and the regulatory nature of measures restricting trade and investment in the sector, lend themselves less readily to reciprocal exchange of market access "concessions" (Hoekman and Messerlin, 2000). The challenge for WTO members is thus to develop negotiating modalities that allow governments to use the GATS as a complementary means of pursuing desired domestic reforms, while improving access to foreign markets.

The Uruguay Round is widely seen as having reaped only a modest harvest of bound liberalisation commitments in the services area. The first round of negotiations laid the foundations for future work, putting in place a (still incomplete) framework of rules under which progressive liberalisation could be pursued in subsequent negotiations. For developing countries, the new set of negotiations raises the twin questions of what the negotiating agenda should be, and how the multilateral process can best be harnessed to make it more conducive to the realisation of development objectives.

The most obvious deficiency of the GATS at present is the number and quality of liberalisation commitments. In many WTO members' national schedules, the sectoral coverage of commitments is small and many of the commitments that do exist are either subject to important limitations or fail even to lock in the statutory or regulatory *status quo*. Such deficiencies are most acute in developing countries, though the scope for broadening and deepening the level of liberalisation of trade and investment is also significant in developed countries.

One reason for the reluctance of governments to lock in reform programmes has been a perceived need to protect incumbent suppliers from immediate competition, either because of "infant industry" arguments or to facilitate "orderly adjustment". Yet the observed failure of infant industry policies lies to an important degree in the difficulty many governments experience in committing credibly to liberalisation at some future date. This tends to occur either because governments often have a direct stake in the national firm's continued operation, or because they are vulnerable to pressure from interest groups – domestic or foreign – that stand to benefit from continued protection.

To harness the full potential of the GATS, countries should use the opportunity offered by the current negotiations to aim for a significant expansion in the number and coverage of commitments and for the progressive, orderly and adjustment-promoting removal of existing limitations.[22] An important start in this regard could be made in the key area of transport, both maritime and air, where little progress was made in the first round of GATS negotiations. As former WTO Director General Renato Ruggiero aptly noted: "It will be hard to claim that the GATS provides the basic infrastructure for world trade so long as the services that carry the world's goods and service providers are not properly covered by it" (Ruggiero, 1998).

An important further negotiating challenge is for WTO members to be clearer on the economy-wide implications of the liberalisation path they voluntarily embark upon in the GATS context. The first round of negotiations saw a clear bias in commitments towards maintaining the market position of *existing* suppliers (domestic and foreign) rather than facilitating the entry of new competitors. It should be recalled that protecting the privileged status of incumbent suppliers will not often be the most economically rational policy. Indeed, the economic literature shows that larger welfare gains tend to be realised from an increase in competition than from simply a change in ownership, be it from public to private hands or from domestic to foreign, or through a relaxation of restrictions on foreign equity participation in domestic firms (Mattoo, 1999).

The steady erosion of the natural monopoly rationale for regulation, combined with growing awareness of the enabling characteristics of key service industries and mounting empirical evidence on the benefits of competition, make it increasingly hard to justify maintaining restrictions on new entry into domestic service markets.[23] By providing governments an opportunity to pre-commit to future liberalisation, and hence signal to domestic and foreign suppliers that domestic market conditions will be altered in a progressive, adjustment-promoting manner, the GATS provides a potentially important means of overcoming the considerable economic and political pressure that incumbents often exert on domestic policy-making. A pre-commitment to liberalise can also instil a sense of urgency to domestic reform and speed up efforts to develop necessary regulatory and supervisory mechanisms.[24] WTO members, developed and developing, should thus make greater use of the signalling properties of the GATS and, where practicable, promote greater market contestability through new entry in their service markets (Low and Mattoo, 2000; Hoekman and Messerlin, 2000).

Arguments by economists that the WTO can be used as a valuable credibility-bolstering device have however proven less than fully compelling at the negotiating table. In practice, the mercantilist logic of multilateral negotiations suggests that industrialised countries will need to improve export opportunities for developing countries, both within and beyond the services field.

Regardless of the negotiation modalities WTO members agree on (*i.e.* request-offer exchanges or formula-based approaches), priority attention should be given to key "backbone" or "enabling" sectors such as transportation, telecommunications, financial services, distribution and energy, as well as to clusters of related activities that are vital to economic development and to greater participation in the world economy (*e.g.* e-commerce, express delivery services and logistics management). Increasing the efficiency of such service sectors will have major payoffs for WTO members in terms of lower prices, higher quality, timeliness of delivery and greater product differentiation (Nielson *et al.*, 2001).

From a negotiating perspective, such infrastructure services are sectors where enterprises in industrialised countries can be expected to dominate the supply side. Traditional negotiating balance imperatives therefore suggest that services and modes of supply where developing countries have an export interest should also be put on the table. Without such "concessions" or trade-offs, developing countries are unlikely to use the GATS to bind the *status quo* or as a pre-commitment device for planned future reforms.

Potential trade-offs within the ambit of the services negotiations can be readily identified (see Box 3). Perhaps the largest potential area for commercially meaningful trade-offs concerns the liberalisation of mode 4 services trade, which involves the temporary entry of services providers. Although traditionally a sensitive policy area in many OECD countries, labour mobility is one area where incremental progress could be made in the new GATS round.[25] It is also one where opposition within OECD countries is far from monolithic; there are many "user" industries that would benefit from – and clamour loudly for – more liberal temporary entry regimes. The development of coalitions with such industries could help change the *status quo* (OECD, 2001*b*).

Box 3. Addressing the service export priorities of developing countries

There are likely to be significant gains worldwide if restrictions on services exports from developing countries are eliminated. With greater liberalisation, particularly in so-called "mode 4" trade, which involves the temporary movement of services suppliers, many more developing countries could "export" at least the significant labour component of services, particularly in industries such as construction, distribution, transport, health and environmental services.

Perhaps the most striking recent example of a developing country's services export success story is the Indian software industry, which has emerged as a significant supplier to developed country markets. Indian software exports grew from USD 225 million in 1992-93 to USD 2.65 billion in 1998-99, a compound annual growth rate exceeding 50%. The sector accounts for 10.5% of total Indian exports today, up from 2.5% a mere five years ago. It is estimated that two of every five Fortune 500 companies outsourced their software requirements to India last year. In 1999-2000, India exported software-related services to 95 countries. Of the total, 62% of software exports went to North America (United States and Canada), and about a quarter to Europe.

Despite the growing importance of cross-border electronic delivery of software services, the movement of natural persons remains a crucial mode of delivery in the sector. Even though the share of on-shore services in total Indian software exports has been in continuous decline (in 1988, the percentage of on-site development stood at nearly 90%), about 60% of Indian exports are still supplied through the temporary movement of programmers. That is, final services are delivered on-shore at the client's site overseas.

Significant gains can be had from further liberalisation of mode 4 services trade in the ICT sector. There are wide differences in the cost of software development and support. The average cost per line of software code in Switzerland (the most expensive country in the OECD area) exceeds by more than a factor of five that in India, and the average salaries of computer programmers are more than eleven times higher in Switzerland than in India. Even though differences in labour productivity imply that a lower average salary of programmers may not necessarily translate into a lower average cost per line of software code, firms in developed countries that outsource programming activities can achieve significant savings in development and support costs. Against the background of a total market for software services worth about USD 58 billion in the United States, USD 42 billion in Europe and USD 10 billion in Japan, such cost savings could well be substantial. Other gains from trade liberalisation for importing countries include a more competitive market structure for software services, increased choice, as countries may develop a special expertise for certain development or support services, and greater diffusion of knowledge (Mattoo, 2000; Chadha, 1999).

The cross-border supply of health services is another area in which developing countries could become major exporters, either by attracting foreign patients to domestic hospitals and doctors, or by temporarily sending their health personnel

Box 3. **Addressing the service export priorities of developing countries** (*cont.*)

abroad. Several developing countries are preparing strategies to become regional leaders in the health service sector. For example, Jordan has since the early 1990s sought to become the medical centre of the Arab world by creating incentives for national and foreign private investment in the sector. As a result, 11 new private hospitals have started operations, most of them benefiting from state-of-art technology. In Singapore, the Parkway Healthcare Group, which first acquired and managed hospitals domestically, has stepped out into the region through joint ventures with partners in host countries. The Group has or is in the process of setting up joint ventures in India, Indonesia, Malaysia, Sri Lanka and the United Kingdom. It is also setting up a specialised cardiac care centre in London. Another notable example is that of Cuba, whose strategy in recent years has been to develop so-called "health tourism" packages.

Some developing countries, such as China and India, are taking advantage of their traditional medicine to attract foreign consumers. There is, indeed, a large and growing demand worldwide for alternative medicine and increasing numbers of foreigners have sought traditional or alternative medical treatment abroad in recent years. China is also sending medical personnel abroad to acquire new techniques and to disseminate the use of traditional medical practices. It has also entered into joint ventures with partners in the medical profession and has opened traditional medical facilities in more than 20 countries (Zarrilli and Kinnon, 1998).

Allowing FDI and eliminating restrictions to the operation and management of the health sector can help to attract foreign patients. In the recent past, several foreign health-care firms have linked up with Indian companies to set up super-speciality hospitals and polyclinics in the country. This will enable India to earn considerable foreign exchange. Such foreign investments can be expected to improve Indian health standards, help disseminate greater expertise and the most recent medical technology, and retain a larger share of medical practitioners trained at public expense in the country's medical schools and universities. It should also encourage foreign patients to come to India in greater numbers (Zarrilli and Kinnon, 1998).

A major barrier to consumption abroad of medical services is the lack of portability of health insurance. In many OECD countries, reimbursement of medical expenses is limited to licensed, certified facilities located in the home country. The lack of long-term portability of health coverage for retirees from OECD countries is also a major constraint on the expansion of cross-border trade in heath services and the greater participation of developing countries in such trade. In some member countries for instance, medical insurance programmes cover virtually no services delivered abroad. Other members may extend coverage abroad, but only for limited periods (*i.e.* two or three months). This constraint is significant because it tends to deter some elderly persons from travelling or retiring abroad. And those who do retire abroad are often forced to return home for medical care. The potential impact of allowing greater portability could be substantial. According to a recent study by the United Nations and the World Health Organisation, if only 3% of the 100 million elderly persons living in OECD countries retired to developing countries, they would bring with them USD 30-50 billion annually in personal consumption and USD 10-15 billion in medical expenditures (Zarrilli and Kinnon, 1998).

Chapter 9

Concluding Remarks

Reform in services markets has been and will likely continue to be driven primarily by domestic priorities. Reform efforts are indeed almost inherently more sustainable in political and economic terms if they are pursued out of recognition of national self-interest, rather than at the behest of foreigners. Left to domestic discretion, however, reform may never be undertaken in any systemic way. Multilateral rule-making and liberalisation efforts can play an essential role in this regard, by helping countries overcome domestic resistance to change and by offering compensatory bargains in sectors of priority export interest. Trade agreements also perform the useful function of allowing countries periodically to lock in past reform efforts. By giving greater permanency to reform efforts, and establishing a floor of openness under conditions of heightened regulatory transparency, bound liberalisation commitments in the services area can send a powerful signal to domestic and foreign suppliers alike. On balance, such signals are likely to generate greater inflows of foreign investment, given the importance of commercial presence as a means of contesting services markets.

The GATS can also serve a central adjustment-enabling function, by allowing WTO members to pre-commit to future liberalisation in an orderly, progressive, manner. Once again, this will tend to send strong signals to incumbents about the need to prepare for a more competitive environment, and to regulatory authorities to put in place a proper regulatory framework to accompany liberalisation efforts and address potential downsides or market failures.

Scheduled liberalisation is not the only yardstick to assess the importance of the GATS for WTO members. From the perspective of an individual economy, whether developed or developing, even standstill bindings are economically and commercially meaningful, given their positive effects on transparency and predictability and, in turn, on investment. This study has drawn attention to the "development-friendliness" of the GATS. This attribute is important in that it allows WTO members considerable flexibility as regards the pace, sequence and nature of services reform and liberalisation efforts they seek to bind voluntarily under the GATS. Such flexibility, and the emphasis in the GATS on the progressive character of market opening efforts, may be of considerable importance in helping countries anticipate, mitigate or avoid potential downsides flowing from liberalisation.

Much hard work lies ahead to complete the work set in motion by the first round of services negotiations. On the rule-making front, this is notably the case with regard to the possible adoption of a GATS-specific emergency safeguard mechanism. WTO members will also need to give continued attention to the areas of subsidies, government procurement and domestic regulation, with a view to determining the scope for any necessary new disciplines in these areas.

On the liberalisation front, an important issue facing WTO members is how best to induce countries to use the GATS as a device to support domestic reforms deemed beneficial from a development perspective by governments and civil society. One of the most urgent priorities confronting negotiators is a significant expansion of the sectoral coverage of liberalisation commitments. Otherwise, the GATS is unlikely to fulfil its complementary role in support of pro-competitive and development-enhancing reforms. Services are one area where the potential gains from international co-operation are large and where the benefits of such co-operation have barely begun to be tapped.

There remains, additionally, the important matter of responding credibly to those who oppose the pursuit of liberalisation of trade and investment under the GATS. A paradox of the anti-GATS crusade is that much of it is rooted in the OECD area, where the share of services in employment and the standards of living are highest and where the benefits of regulatory reform and liberalisation of trade and investment in services have arguably generated the greatest gains in consumer welfare and allocative efficiencies. Not surprisingly, the public policy debate on services in OECD countries has tended to centre not so much on disputing the economic case for open markets. Rather, GATS critics have focused on the respective roles that the market and the state (as both regulator and direct purveyor of services such as education and health) should be assuming, as well on the threat to national regulatory sovereignty allegedly posed by trade and investment rule-making.

This agenda differs quite significantly from that in many developing countries, where a reluctance to embrace more readily the liberalisation of services trade and investment in a GATS setting (even as such liberalisation is practised domestically) can be traced to a combination of factors. These include tactical bargaining considerations in the WTO as well as the power of vested interests in government and in import-competing sectors (including in some instances foreign firms enjoying dominant market positions). However, it also reflects the legitimate concerns of many developing countries regarding their lack of appropriate regulatory regimes and institutions, weak technical capacities, poor market information, difficulties in meeting product standards in export markets, continued restrictions on temporary labour mobility in export markets, and the need for significant upgrading of human resources. Such ingredients are required to make a success of liberalisation, and their absence or relative paucity may constrain the ability of many developing countries to supply services in export markets, even where demand for such services may exist (UNCTAD, 1999*a*).

The two agendas described above are not easily reconciled, as this study, which has addressed the GATS debate as it arises in member and non-member alike, has brought out.

To sum up, the multilateral community faces a dual challenge in the current GATS round. A first challenge consists of responding credibly to the rising chorus of criticisms levelled at the GATS. There can be little doubt that even as such concerns are legitimately felt and expressed, they are in many instances greatly exaggerated and demonstrate a misunderstanding of the aims and operation of the GATS. The ongoing negotiations provide a ready-made opportunity for governments to inform concerned constituencies about the GATS and how it affects national economic and social goals.

A second challenge is to build support among all WTO members, and especially developing countries, for wider and more commercially meaningful GATS commitments. Liberalisation under the GATS will nonetheless remain progressive in character, and will in many instances require concomitant efforts at capacity building in education, training, institutional and regulatory matters. To make a success of the GATS negotiations, efforts will also be needed to progressively open up areas of export interest to developing countries, notably in sectors such as construction, tourism and travel-related services, computer services, as well as in respect of the movement of service suppliers, so-called "mode 4" trade in services.

In concluding, a word of caution seems in order. It is important that the relative contribution of liberalisation of trade and investment to ongoing structural change be properly understood, and set against other forces, chief among which is technology, that are reshaping the world's economic landscape. In stating the case for open markets, it bears recalling that liberalisation of trade and investment are means of helping societies and individuals cope with change and take advantage of the opportunities afforded by closer economic integration. Liberalisation is never, nor should it be, an end in itself.

At the same time, stakeholders in the public debate over market openness should guard against the tendency to expect – and at times promise – more than liberalisation of trade and investment can realistically be expected to deliver. Just as unhelpful is the tendency to ascribe to trade and investment policy a greater influence on countries' and citizens' destinies than is warranted relative to more purely domestic or independent forces and the sovereign exercise of policy choices.

The above considerations do not, of course, take away from the positive overall effects of open services markets on the welfare of nations and the pocketbooks of citizens. Because they are the backbone of a vibrant market economy, the case for open services markets is just as strong – if not stronger – than that for goods trade. It matters greatly therefore that governments should be able to communicate the case in favour of open services markets, make clear what is and is not subject to trade disciplines and negotiations, and explain why and how a sustained commitment to international co-operation and to open markets more often than not forms part of the answer to the concerns of their citizens, rather than being their root cause (OECD, 1998).

Notes

1. See Hill (1977); Krommenacker (1979); Sapir and Lutz (1981); Bhagwati (1984); Commission of the European Communities (1984); Hindley and Smith (1984); Sampson and Snape (1985); Riddle (1986); Nusbaumer (1987); Giarini (1987); Office of Technology Assessment (1987); Kakabadse (1987); Feketekuty (1988); Nicolaidis (1989).

2. In order to benefit from the process of globalisation and its attendant "splintering" or "fragmentation" of the production chain, enterprises must have access to efficient service inputs. As nations have reduced tariffs and other barriers to trade, effective rates of protection for manufacturing industries may become negative if the latter are confronted with input prices that are higher than they would be if services markets were open to competition.

3. Recent theoretical research (Deardorff, 1999; Markusen *et al.*, 1999) shows that there are strong reasons to believe that liberalisation of such services deserves priority in the negotiations because they are crucial in terms both of increasing the gains from trade in goods and of reducing the costs of international fragmentation of the value chain and production sharing.

4. See Francois and Wooton (1999) for recent studies on maritime transport. Findlay and Warren (1999) present a series of papers exploring the magnitude of barriers to trade in telecommunications, financial and other services.

5. The openness index for telecommunications used by the authors captures the degree of competition, restrictions on ownership and the existence of an independent regulator; it draws on a database developed jointly by the International Telecommunications Union (ITU) and World Bank for 1998. The index for financial services captures restrictions on new entry, restrictions on foreign ownership and capital mobility; it draws primarily on commitments made by countries under the GATS which are known to reflect actual policy and data in the International Monetary Fund's (IMF) Annual Report on Exchange Arrangements and Exchange Restrictions.

6. The question of an emergency safeguard measure (ESM) in services trade has been on the GATS agenda for several years now. The debate has evolved but still appears somewhat elusive, as reflected in the decision by GATS members to extend for a third time, to 15 March 2002, the deadline for completing negotiations on an ESM. The desirability of an ESM remains very much an open question, given the state of our knowledge of services trade. The test of "unforeseen circumstances" which is instrumental to the consideration of an ESM, remains fragile, simply because it is difficult to understand how it can be made operational via objective tests. Even if the desirability is accepted, one must consider feasibility when it is apparent that there are several hurdles to overcome, such as: modes of delivery, particularly commercial presence; determining the "likeness" of services and service providers; the impact of technology; the

general paucity of statistical information required for credible injury determinations as well as the diversity of trade interests at stake (for instance, the fear of some developing countries that mode 4 trade might be particularly vulnerable to ESMs).

7. A recurring concern in the debate over liberalisation concerns the possible reduction in employment in formerly public monopolies, which have frequently employed surplus labour. For example, a study by Alexander and Estache (1999) finds that the privatisation of electricity distribution in Argentina led to a 40% decline in the workforce after privatisation. But there is also evidence that pessimism over the employment effects of liberalisation may not always be justified. For example, a number of developing countries have managed to maintain or even increase employment in their liberalised telecommunications sectors. Petrazzini and Lovelock (1996) find, in a study of 26 Latin American and Asian economies, that telecommunication markets with competition were the only ones that consistently increased employment levels, while two-thirds of the countries with monopolies saw considerable declines in their telecommunications workforce.

8. However, although there may be proportionately fewer low-skilled workers (*i.e.* potential "losers" from import competition) in the service sector, given that the sector accounts for close to 70% of most OECD economies, the number of negatively affected workers may still be significant relative to those in manufacturing.

9. The magazine *Foreign Policy*, in partnership with A. T. Kearney, has developed a Globalisation Index which attempts to measure globalisation by quantifying what it considers to be the key indicators. It takes into account measurement of international trade and convergence of domestic and world prices, capital and investment flows, Internet connectivity and movement of persons across national borders. Its objective is to gauge the extent and speed of the spread of globalisation and to be able to estimate how "global" a given country is. A.T. Kearney/*Foreign Policy* finds that while the debate on the subject is "unsatisfactory" – notably because until now no attempt has been made to measure globalisation – in terms of definition: "there seems to be a consensus that globalisation – whether economic, political, cultural or environmental – is defined by increasing levels of interdependence over vast distances". See the Foreign Policy Web site: *www.foreignpolicy.com*

10. Translated from excerpts from a speech given 6 April 2001, "Maîtriser la mondialisation", *Les Echos*, 10 April 2001.

11. See the organisation's Web site: *www.cupe.ca/mediaroom/newsreleases/showitem.asp?id=*87.

12. This is not to say that a binding produces an absolute and irrevocable commitment. GATS provides means by which countries can condition or even suspend a commitment for legitimate reasons of public policy.

13. Preamble to the GATS; see also WTO, "The GATS: objectives, coverage and disciplines", available on the WTO Web site: *www.wto.org*.

14. Contrary to claims often made by non-governmental groups active in the environmental field, the market access provisions of the GATS (Article XVI) allow WTO members (at the federal or sub-national level) to place quantitative limitations on potentially environmentally harmful service operations relating for instance to oil and gas extraction, oil and gas pipelines or waste incinerators.

15. The "prudential carve-out" provisions contained in the GATS Annex on Financial Services are worthy of note in any discussion of the impact of the GATS on domestic

regulation. Article 2 of the Annex provides that, notwithstanding any other GATS provisions, member countries may implement prudential measures to protect consumers and/or to ensure the stability and security of their financial systems, so long as these measures are not used to avoid commitments. Members are encouraged to recognise, on a bilateral or multilateral basis, the prudential measures of other countries and take them into account in applying their own measures, provided that all countries are eligible for such recognition. In recognition of the critical importance of financial stability, the GATS also contains specific provisions that preserve and emphasise the right of governments to intervene in the management of the sector. For instance, the activities of central banks and related monetary authorities in the pursuit of monetary or exchange rate policies, and macroeconomic management in general, are specifically excluded from the scope of the Agreement. The same applies to activities forming part of a statutory system of social security or public retirement plans.

16. The WTO secretariat has itself recently noted that, given the attention accorded to the "public services carve out" clause in the public debate, the new set of negotiations provides a good opportunity to "make it clear that the co-existence of governmental and private services in the same industry does not mean that they are in competition in the sense of Article I(3)(c) of GATS and therefore does not invalidate the exclusion from the GATS of the public sector" (WTO, 2001*b*).

17. The three WTO members that have put forward negotiating proposals on trade in education services are Australia, New Zealand and the United States (WTO, 2001*c*, *d* and *e*).

18. A number of general principles common to international investment agreements (and other agreements such as the GATT) govern the provision of services via a commercial presence under the GATS. Non-discrimination – provided for by MFN treatment and national treatment obligations – and transparency are two fundamental GATS principles. Free transfer of payments and policy lock-in (where commitments are scheduled) are also contained in the GATS. However, the GATS does not deal with some important disciplines that are traditionally included in investment agreements, such as investment incentives, performance requirements, protection against expropriation or compensation. Nor does it allow private parties direct recourse to the WTO's dispute settlement provisions, an issue that has garnered considerable attention in the North American Free Trade Agreement (NAFTA) context, as it did in the Multilateral Agreement on Investment (MAI) negotiations.

19. Little progress has been made to date beyond preliminary discussions of conceptual issues and first attempts at assessing subsidy impacts in a GATS setting (WTO, 2001). This reflects both the complexity and sensitivity of the issues at stake, including the fact that, in many countries, subsidies are granted at the sub-national level. Given the current state of discussions, it is not possible to assess the impact of any future set of possible subsidy disciplines under the GATS. Many issues would need to be considered before such disciplines could be negotiated: the important role that subsidies can play in establishing viable service industries in developing countries; the relevance of the WTO's Subsidies and Countervailing Measures (SCM) Agreement; the desirability of introducing disciplines on investment incentives. In addition, the particularities of services trade, notably the multiple modes of supply, mean that a direct transposition of concepts developed for goods trade under the SCM Agreement would be hard to effect in a GATS context.

20. It should be noted that the negotiating mandate on subsidies under GATS Article XV relates solely to the potentially distortive effects that may be caused by subsidies and not to the granting of subsidies *per se*.

21. For example, Article V(3) on economic integration; Article XIX (2); and the technical co-operation provisions (Article 6) of the Annex on Telecommunications.

22. Setting targets for expanding the coverage to be achieved in the next round would help provide a focal point for policy makers. Quantitative indicators that could be considered include the share of sectors that have been scheduled, and the share of commitments that involve a bound promise not to apply any national treatment or market access violating measures. Neither indicator requires any judgement regarding the importance of actual policies that restrict national treatment or market access, whether or not scheduled (Thompson, 2001). One problem with formula-based approaches to expanding coverage is that sectors that are important inputs into production and sectors where barriers to trade and investment are currently highest may remain excluded in both developed and developing countries. Consequently, request-offer negotiations of the type used in the first round of GATS talks cannot and should not be avoided.

23. An industry is said to be a natural monopoly when a single firm can supply a good or a service to an entire market at a smaller cost than could two or more firms. A natural monopoly arises when there are economies of scale over the relevant range of output. Telecommunications and electricity supply are two industries that were long thought to be natural monopolies. However, technological change (*e.g.* the advent of mobile telephony) and the unbundling of markets (*e.g.* power production and distribution; access to and use of telecommunications networks), by making competitive entry feasible, have gradually eroded the rationale for maintaining monopolistic market structures in both sectors in most countries.

24. During recent GATS-based negotiations on basic telecommunications and financial services, several governments took advantage of the GATS to balance their reluctance to unleash competition immediately on protected national suppliers, and their desire not to be held hostage in perpetuity either to the weakness of domestic industry or to pressure from vested interests. This was most striking in the case of basic telecommunications, where a number of African, Latin American and Caribbean countries bound themselves to introduce competition at precise future dates. For several countries, this signalled the end of the exclusive rights granted for many years to a foreign monopolist or dominant supplier. The GATS has been less widely used as a mechanism for lending credibility to financial sector liberalisation programmes, in part because financial services markets tend to be more competitive than basic telecommunications and because the negotiations were concluded at a time of considerable uncertainty in financial markets (Mattoo, 2000).

25. This is particularly so as one of the key instruments used to restrict trade through this mode of supply involves quantity-based policy tools (through visa quotas). These can be expanded over time, with "within quota" visas not being subject to economic needs tests, and possibly with liberalisation facilitated by a safeguard procedure specific to mode 4. For detailed proposals by developing country scholars in this area, see Chanda (1999) and Mukherjee (1999). Further information on the scheduling of economic needs tests under both mode 3 (commercial presence) and mode 4 (movement of natural persons) of the GATS can be found in Morris (2001).

References

Adlung, R. (2000),
"Services Trade Liberalization from Developed and Developing Country Perspectives", in P. Sauvé and R. M. Stern (eds.), GATS 2000: *New Directions in Services Trade Liberalization*, Washington, DC: Brookings Institution Press and Center for Business and Government, Harvard University, pp. 112-131.

Alexander, I. and A. Estache (1999),
"The Role of Regulatory Reform and Growth: Lessons from Latin America", paper presented at TIPS Annual Forum, Johannesburg, South Africa, September.

APEC (1998*a*),
"The Impact of Liberalisation: Telecommunications Industry in the Philippines" (November), Singapore: APEC Secretariat, available at *www.apec.org*

APEC (1998*b*),
"The Impact of Liberalisation: Financial Service Sector in Peru" (November), Singapore: APEC Secretariat, available at *www.apec.org*

Ascher, B. (2001),
"Education and Training Services in International Trade Agreements", paper prepared for a Conference on Higher Education and Training in the Global Marketplace: Exporting Issues and Trade Agreements, sponsored by the Center for Quality Assurance in International Education and the US Department of Commerce, Washington, DC, 10 May.

Azad, A. K. (1999),
"Inter-Industry Linkages of Services in the Bangladesh Economy (with a Case Study of the Ready-made Garments Industry) and Potential Services Trade", mimeo, Washington, DC: The World Bank.

Babe, R. (1996),
"Convergence and New Technologies", in M. Dorland (ed.), *The Cultural Industries in Canada: Problems, Policies, and Prospects*, Toronto: James Lorimer and Company.

Barajas, A., R. Steiner and N. Salazar (2000),
"Foreign Investment in Colombia's Financial Sector", in S. Claessens and M. Jansen (eds.), *The Internationalization of Financial Services: Issues and Lessons for Developing Countries*, London: Kluwer Law International, pp. 355-388.

Bertrand, A. (2000),
L'Observatoire de la mondialisation, in "L'OMC à l'assaut des services", *Libération*, 6 October.

Bhagwati, J. (1984),
"Splintering and Disembodiment of Services and Developing Nations", in *The World Economy*, Vol. 7, No. 2, pp. 133-143.

Bishop, T. (1996),
"France and the Need for Cultural Exception", *New York University Journal of International Law and Politics*, Vol. 29, Nos. 1-2.

Centre for Research on Globalisation and Labour Markets (2000),
"Multinationals and Export Spillovers", Research Paper 2000/14.

Chadha, R. (1999),
"GATS and Developing Countries: A Case Study of India", mimeo, New Delhi: National Center for Advanced Economic Research.

Chambre de Commerce et d'Industrie de Paris (2001),
"La libéralisation des services à l'OMC: intérêts des exportateurs français", Paris: Chambre de Commerce et d'Industrie de Paris, 28 June.

Chanda, R. (1999),
"Movement of Natural Persons and Trade in Services: Liberalising Temporary Movement of Labour under the GATS", mimeo, New Delhi: Indian Council for Research on International Economic Relations.

Chen, S. (2001),
"Structural Changes and Canada's Trade and Investment in Services", mimeo, Ottawa: Department of Foreign Affairs and International Trade.

Claessens, S. and M. Jansen (eds.) (2000),
The Internationalization of Financial Services: Issues and Lessons for Developing Countries, London: Kluwer Law International.

Commission of the European Communities (1984),
Study on International Trade in Services, Brussels: EC Commission.

Commission of the European Communities (1996*a*),
"The 1996 Single Market Review", Commission Staff Working Paper, Brussels: Commission of the European Communities.

Commission of the European Communities (1996*b*),
"Road Freight Transport", Single Market Review Series, Sub-series II – Impact on Services, Brussels: Commission of the European Communities, March.

Copeland, B. R. (2001),
"Benefits and Costs of Trade and Investment Liberalisation in Services: Implications from Trade Theory", paper prepared for the Department of Foreign Affairs and International Trade, Government of Canada.

Deardorff, A. (1999),
"International Provision of Trade Services, Trade and Fragmentation", mimeo, Ann Arbor: University of Michigan.

Dee, P. and K. Hanslow (1999),
"Multilateral Liberalisation of Services Trade", Canberra: Australian Productivity Commission.

Dorland, M. (ed.) (1996),
The Cultural Industries in Canada: Problems, Policies, and Prospects, Toronto: James Lorimer and Company.

Education International (2000),
"The WTO and the Millennium Round – What is at Stake for Public Education", May, available at *www.ei-ie.org*.

Federal Communications Commission (1999),
Trends in the US International Telecommunications Industry, Washington, DC: Federal Communications Commission.

Feketekuty, G. (1988),
International Trade in Services: An Overview and Blueporint for Negotiations, The American Enterprise Institute Trade in Services Series, Cambridge, Massachusetts: Ballinger Press.

Findlay, C. and T. Warren (eds.) (2000),
Impediments to Trade in Services: Measurement and Policy Implications, Sydney: Routledge.

Fink, C., A. Mattoo and I. C. Neagu (2001),
"Trade in International Maritime Services: How Much Does Policy Matter?", World Bank Working Paper 2522, Washington, DC: The World Bank.

Francois, J. and B. Hoekman (1999),
"Market Access in the Service sectors", mimeo, Washington, DC: The World Bank.

Francois, J. and I. Wooton (1999),
"Trade in International Transport Services: The Role of Competition", mimeo, Rotterdam: Tinbergen Institute, Erasmus University.

Gauthier, G. *et al.* (2000),
"Déjà Vu, or New Beginning for Safeguards and Subsidies Rules in Services Trade", in P. Sauvé and R. M. Stern (eds.), GATS 2000: *New Directions in Services Trade Liberalization*, Washington, DC: Brookings Institution Press and Center for Business and Government, Harvard University, pp. 165-183.

Giarini, O. (ed.) (1987),
The Emerging Service Economy, Oxford: Pergamon Press.

Graham, E. M. (2000),
Fighting the Wrong Enemy: Antiglobal Activists and Multinational Enterprises, Washington, DC: Institute for International Economics.

Hartridge, D. (2000),
"Service Trade and Globalisation – Government Services and Public Policy Concerns", speech given to the European Services Forum, Brussels, 27 November.

Heeks, R. (1998),
"The Uneven Profile of Indian Software Exports", Development Informatics Working Paper No. 3, Institute for Development Policy and Management, University of Manchester *www.man.ac.uk/idpm/diwpf3.htm*.

Hill, T. P. (1977),
"On Goods and Services", in *The Review of Income and Wealth*, Vol. 23, No. 4, pp. 315-338.

Hindley, B. and A. Smith (1984),
"Comparative Advantage and Trade in Services", in *The World Economy*, Vol. 7, No. 4, pp. 369-389.

Hodge, J. (1998),
"Examining the Cost of Services Protection in a Developing Country: The Case of South Africa", paper prepared for the World Services Congress, Atlanta, November.

Hoekman, B. (2001)
"Strengthening the Global Trade Architecture for Development", mimeo, Washington, DC: The World Bank, 17 August.

Hoekman, B. and A. Mattoo (1999)
"Services, Economic Development and the Next Round of Negotiations on Services", *Journal of International Development*, Vol. 12, pp. 283-296.

Hoekman, B. and D. Konan (1999)
"Deep Integration, Non-Discrimination and Euro-Mediterranean Free Trade", London: CEPR Discussion Paper 2095.

Hoekman, B. and P. Messerlin (2000)
"Liberalizing Trade in Services: Reciprocal Negotiations and Regulatory Reform", in P. Sauvé and R. M. Stern (eds.), GATS 2000: *New Directions in Services Trade Liberalization*, Washington, DC: Brookings Institution Press and Center for Business and Government, Harvard University, pp. 487-508.

Hufbauer, G. C. and C. Findlay (eds.) (1996)
Flying High: Liberalizing Civil Aviation in the Asia Pacific, Washington, DC: Institute for International Economics.

Hufbauer, G. C. and T. Warren (1999),
"The Globalization of Services: What Has Happened? What Are the Implications?", mimeo, Washington, DC: Institute for International Economics.

Infometrics Consulting (2000),
"Economic Impact Analysis of Foreign fee-Paying Students", report prepared for the New Zealand International Education Marketing Network, Wellington.

International Telecommunication Union (2000*a*),
"Key Indicators for the World Telecommunication Service Sector", Geneva: International Telecommunication Union, available at *www/itu.int*

International Telecommunication Union (2000*b*),
America's Telecommunication Indicators 2000, Geneva: International Telecommunication Union, April.

Jayarante, J. and P. E. Strahan (1996),
"The Finance-Growth Nexus: Evidence from Bank Branch Deregulation", in *Quarterly Journal of Economics*, No. 111, pp. 639-670.

Juillard, P. (2000),
A *propos du décès de l'*AMI, Cours de la Hague, Blackwell Publishers.

Kakabadse, M. (1987),
"International Trade in Services", Atlantic Paper No. 64, Paris: Atlantic Institute for International Affairs.

Karsenty, Guy (2000),
"Assessing Trade in Services by Mode of Supply", in P. Sauvé and R. M. Stern (eds.), GATS 2000: *New Directions in Services Trade Liberalization*, Washington, DC: Brookings Institution Press and Center for Business and Government, Harvard University, pp. 33-56.

Kirkman, G. (1999),
"It's More Than Just Being Connected: A Discussion of Some Issues of Information Technology and International Development", paper presented at the Development E-Commerce Workshop, Cambridge, Massachusetts: The Media Laboratory at the Massachusetts Institute of Technology, 16-17 April. See: *www.cid.harvard.edu/cidtrade/*

Kletzer, L. (2001),
"Measuring the Costs of Trade-related Job Losses", testimony prepared for the United States Senate Committee on Finance, 20 July, available at *www.iiw.com/papers/kletzer0701.htm*

Konan, D. and Maskus, K. (2000),
"Service Liberalization in WTO 2000: A Computable General Equilibrium Model of Tunisia", mimeo, Washington, DC: The World Bank.

Krommenacker, R. (1979),
"Trade Related Services and GATT", in *Journal of World Trade Law*, Vol. 13, No. 6 (November-December).

Lee, N.C. and Lie, H.Y. (2000),
"Korea's Telecom Services Reform through Trade Negotiations", research paper, Seoul: Korea Information Society Development Institute.

Low, P. and A. Mattoo (2000),
"Is There a Better Way? Alternative Approaches to Liberalization Under GATS", in P. Sauvé and R. M. Stern (eds.), GATS 2000: *New Directions in Services Trade Liberalization*, Washington, DC: Brookings Institution Press and Center for Business and Government, Harvard University, pp. 449-472.

Mander, J. and J. Goldsmith (eds.) (1996),
The Case Against the Global Economy, San Francisco: Sierra Club Books.

Mann, C. (2000),
Global Electronic Commerce: A Policy Primer, Washington, DC: Institute for International Economics.

Maris, B. (2000),
"Libéraliser, sans avoir l'air d'y toucher", in *Le Monde Diplomatique*, July.

Markusen, J. R. (1989),
"Trade in Producer Services and in Other Specialized Intermediate Inputs", in *American Economic Review*, Vol. 79, pp. 85-95.

Markusen, J. R., T. Rutherford and D. Tarr (1999),
"Foreign Direct Investment in Services and the Domestic Market for Expertise", mimeo, Washington, DC: The World Bank.

Mattoo, A. (1999),
"Developing Countries in the New Round of GATS Negotiations: From a Defensive to a Proactive Role", mimeo, Washington, DC: The World Bank, March. *www1.worldbank.org/wbiep/trade/services/services_ldc_wecon.pdf*

Mattoo, A. (2000),
"Financial Services and the WTO: Liberalization Commitments of the Developing and Transition Economies", in *The World Economy*, Vol. 23, No. 4, pp. 471-489.

Mattoo, A., R. Rathindran and A. Subramanian (2001),
"Measuring Services Trade Liberalization and its Impact on Economic Growth: An Illustration", World Bank Research Working Paper, No. 2655, Washington, DC: The World Bank.

Moore, M. (2001),
"Freer Trade Can Empower the Internet and Close the Divide", in *The International Herald Tribune*, 7 June.

Morris, R. (2001),
"The Scheduling of Economic Needs Tests in the GATS: An Overview", in *Trade in Services: Negotiating Issues and Approaches*, Paris: OECD.

Mukherjee, N. (1999),
"Market Access Commitments under GATS: An Analysis from Developing Countries' Perspective", paper prepared for the World Services Congress, Atlanta, Georgia, November.

Nader, R. and L. Wallach (1996),
"NAFTA and the Subversion of Democratic Process", in J. Mander and J. Goldsmith (eds.), *The Case Against the Global Economy*, San Francisco: Sierra Club Books.

Naim, M. (2001),
"New Economy, Old Politics", in *Foreign Affairs*, Spring.

Nicolaidis, P. (1989),
"Liberalizing Service Trade: Strategies for Success", Chatham House Papers, London: The Royal Institute of International Affairs.

Nicoletti, G. (2001),
"Regulation in Services: OECD Patterns and Economic Implications", Economics Department Working Papers No. 287, Paris: OECD, 8 February.

Nielson, J., C. Pellegrino, R. Morris and R. Thompson (2001),
"Using Cluster Approaches to Specific Commitments for Interdependent Services", in *Trade in Services: Negotiating Issues and Approaches*, Paris: OECD.

Nusbaumer, J. (1987),
Services in the Global Market, Boston: Kluwer.

OECD (1998),
Open Markets Matter: The Benefits of Trade and Investment Liberalisation, Paris: OECD.

OECD (1999),
"A Review of Market Openness and Trade in Telecommunications", DSTI/ICCP/TISP/(99)5/FINAL, Paris.

OECD (2000*a*),
Cellular Mobile Pricing Structures and Trends, Paris: OECD.

OECD (2000*b*),
Education at a Glance, Paris: OECD.

OECD (2000*c*),
Understanding the Digital Divide, Paris: OECD.

OECD (2001*a*),
Trade in Services: Negotiating Issues and Approaches, Paris: OECD.

OECD (2001*b*),
"Service Providers on the Move: A Close Look at Labour Mobility and the GATS", TD/TC/WP(2002)26, Paris.

OECD (2001*c*),
The Well-being of Nations –The Role of Human and Social Capital, Paris: OECD/CERI.

OECD (2000*a*),
Cellular Mobile Pricing Structures and Trends, Paris: OECD.

Office of Technology Assessment (1987),
International Competition in Services, Washington, DC: Congress of the United States, Office of Technology Assessment.

Olson, M. (1965),
The Logic of Collective Action, Cambridge, Massachusetts: Harvard University Press.

Petrazzini, B. A. and P. Lovelock (1996),
"Telecommunications in the Region: Comparative Case Studies", paper presented at the International Institute for Telecommunications Forum, Sydney, Australia, 22-23 April.

Productivity Commission (1998),
"International Air Services – Inquiry Report", Canberra: Productivity Commission, 11 September, available at *www.pc.gov.au/inquiry/airserv/finalrep/index.html*

Productivity Commission (2000),
Achieving Better Regulation of Services, Conference Proceedings, Canberra: Productivity Commission and Australian National University.

Riddle, D. (1986),
Service-led Growth: The Role of the Service Sector in World Development, New York: Praeger.

Roseman Associates (2001),
"Economic Impact of Trade and Investment Liberalisation in the Telecommunications Sector: A Review of Literature for Selected Countries", mimeo, Ottawa: Department for Foreign Affairs and International Trade, 30 March.

Ruggiero, R. (1998),
"Towards GATS 2000 – A European Strategy", address to the Conference on Trade in Services organised by the European Commission, Brussels, 2 June.

Sampson, G. and R. Snape (1985),
"Identifying Issues in Trade in Services", in *The World Economy*, Vol. 8, No. 2, pp. 171-181.

Sapir, A. and E. Lutz (1981),
"Trade in Services: Economic Determinants and Development-Related Issues", in *World Bank Staff Working Papers*, No. 480, Washington, DC: The World Bank.

Sauvé, P. (2000),
"Developing Countries and the GATS 2000 Round", *Journal of World Trade*, Vol. 34, No. 2, April, pp. 85-92.

Sauvé, P. (2001*a*),
"The Unfinished Business of GATS: Addressing Uruguay Round Leftovers", mimeo, Washington, DC: The World Bank.

Sauvé, P. (2001*b*),
"Scaling Back Ambitions on Investment Rule-Making at the WTO", *Journal of World Investment*, Vol. 2, No. 3, September, pp. 529-36.

Sauvé, P. and C. Wilkie (2000),
"Investment Liberalisation in GATS," in P. Sauvé and R. M. Stern (eds.), GATS 2000: *New Directions in Services Trade Liberalization*, Washington, DC: Brookings Institution Press and Center for Business and Government, Harvard University, pp. 331-363.

Sauvé, P. and R. M. Stern (eds.), (2000),
GATS 2000: *New Directions in Services Trade Liberalization*, Washington, DC: Brookings Institution Press and Center for Business and Government, Harvard University.

Service Industry Trends (2001),
"Bermuda's Phone Calls down by 66 Percent", 13 May, available at *www.sitrends.org*

Sinclair, S. (2000),
"How the World Trade Organisation's New 'Services' Negotiations Threaten Democracy", Ottawa: Canadian Centre for Policy Alternatives.

Thompson, R. (2001),
"Cross-cutting ('Formula') Approaches to Multilateral Services Negotiations", in *Trade in Services: Negotiating Issues and Approaches*, Paris: OECD.

UNCTAD (1999*a*),
"Assessment of Trade in Services of Developing Countries: Summary of Findings", a note by the UNCTAD Secretariat, UNCTAD/ITCD/TSB/7 (16 August), Geneva: United Nations Conference on Trade and Development.

UNCTAD (1999*b*),
"Analysis of Experiences in Selected Service Sectors", a note by the UNCTAD Secretariat, Geneva: United Nations Conference on Trade and Development.

UNCTAD (2000),
World Investment Report 2000 – *Cross-Border Mergers and Acquisitions and Development*, Geneva: United Nations Conference on Trade and Development.

United States Department of State (2000),
"FY 2001 Country Commercial Guide: Philippines", July, Bureau of Economic and Business Affairs, available at *www.state.gov/*

Van Grasstek, C. (2001),
"Globalized Trade in Services: The Benefits for Consumers, Producers and Society", mimeo, Washington, DC: Washington Trade Reports.

Van Leeuwen, F. (2000),
"Education and the Wealth of Nations", in *Education International Quarterly*, Vol. 6, No. 1.

Wellenius, B. (2000),
"Extending Telecommunications Service to Rural Areas – The Chilean Experience: Awarding Subsidies through Competitive Bidding", mimeo, Washington, DC: The World Bank.

World Bank (1999),
Entering the 21st Century – World Development Report 1999/2000, Oxford University Press.

World Bank (2001),
"Global Economic Prospects and the Developing Countries 2002 – Making Trade Work for the World's Poor", Washington, DC: The World Bank, 11 October.

World Trade Organization (1997),
"Economic Effects of Services Liberalisation", background note by the Secretariat, S/C/W/26 (7 October), Geneva: World Trade Organization.

World Trade Organization (1998*a*),
"Economic Effects of Services Liberalisation: Overview of Empirical Studies", background note by the Secretariat, S/C/W/26/Add.1 (29 May), Geneva: World Trade Organization.

World Trade Organization (1998*b*),
"Telecommunications Services", background note by the Secretariat, S/C/W/74, Geneva: World Trade Organization.

World Trade Organization (1998*c*),
"Health and Social Services", background note by the Secretariat, S/C/W/50, Geneva: World Trade Organisation.

World Trade Organization (1999*a*),
"Assessment of Trade in Services – Japan's Non-Paper", S/C/W/105, Geneva: World Trade Organization.

World Trade Organization (1999*b*),
"The Developmental Impact of Trade Liberalization Under GATS", Job No. 2748/Rev. 1, Geneva: World Trade Organization.

World Trade Organization (2000),
Annual Report, International Trade Statistics, Geneva: World Trade Organization.

World Trade Organization (2001*a*),
Market Access: Unfinished Business – Post-Uruguay Round Inventory and Issues, Special Study No. 6 (27 April), Geneva: World Trade Organization.

World Trade Organization (2001*b*),
"GATS: Fact and Fiction", Geneva: World Trade Organization, available at *www.wto.org*

World Trade Organization (2001*c*),
"Communication from Australia – Negotiating Proposal for Education Services", S/CSS/W/110 (1 October), Geneva: World Trade Organization.

World Trade Organization (2001*d*),
"Communication from New Zealand – Negotiating Proposal for Education Services", S/CSS/W/93 (26 June), Geneva: World Trade Organization.

World Trade Organization (2001e),
"Communication from the United States – Higher (Tertiary) Education, Adult Education and Training", S/CSS/W/23, Geneva: World Trade Organization.

Zarrilli, S. and C. Kinnon (eds.) (1998),
International Trade in Health Services – A Development Perspective, Geneva: United Nations Conference on Trade and Development and World Health Organization.

OECD PUBLICATIONS, 2, rue André-Pascal, 75775 PARIS CEDEX 16
PRINTED IN FRANCE
(22 2002 02 1 P) ISBN 92-64-19725-7 – No. 52419 2002